THE PSYCHOLOGICAL NOVEL

1900 - 1950

THE
PSYCHOLOGICAL
NOVEL
1900-1950

By LEON EDEL

J. B. LIPPINCOTT COMPANY

NEW YORK   PHILADELPHIA

A portion of Chapter III, "The Point of View," appeared originally as Preface (Copyright, 1953, by Leon Edel) to Henry James's The Sacred Fount, *Grove Press, New York, 1953.*

For Roberta

FOREWORD

IN THIS ESSAY I HAVE SOUGHT TO DEFINE WHAT SEEMS TO me the most characteristic aspect of twentieth century fiction: its inward turning to convey the flow of mental experience—what has been called the "stream of consciousness." Actually this essay embraces much more: it is concerned with the manner in which emotional and sensory experience has been rendered in fiction: the bold attempt of certain novelists to make words evoke image and symbol as the poet does—the large effort of certain modern novelists to write symbolist fiction.

An early—a quite primitive—version of this essay was sketched out by me as far back as 1928 under the impulse of a reading of *Ulysses* and the first novels of Virginia Woolf. But the subject then was too "new"; to attempt it was to find oneself in the very laboratory of fiction, amid the puzzles of Joyce's *Work in Progress* which later became *Finnegans Wake,* and the efforts of Mrs. Woolf to write novels about moments of feeling rather than matters of fact. Dorothy Richardson was still absorbed in her *roman fleuve* and Marcel Proust's great work was only beginning to be read in its English form. A critic seeking to understand what was happening to the art of the novel in the 1920's found himself peering along a road that as yet had no ending.

All that now is of the past. Joyce is gone and so is Vir-

7

ginia Woolf. Dorothy Richardson, still among us at an advanced age, has suffered that other death of the artist: she is unread. Proust has become a legend. And William Faulkner has emerged as the successor to these innovators and as a remarkable innovator himself. Instead of peering down an endless road, we look back along that populated highway Miss Richardson imaged when she discovered she was not experimenting alone.

In 1952, when I was invited to give the Christian Gauss Seminar in Criticism at Princeton, it seemed to me that it was now possible to write the essay I had so meagerly adumbrated and laid aside in 1928. I discovered, moreover, that while much brilliant criticism has been written about the individual novelists and their techniques (save Miss Richardson) there had been no systematic appraisal of the modern psychological novel from the high critical ground that permits an unobstructed view. I accordingly devoted the seminar to a discussion of the "stream of consciousness" novel; later this subject was enlarged (during 1953–54 in another seminar at New York University) to a discussion of the contemporary psychological novel.

In a sense this essay might be said to take up the novel where both Percy Lubbock in *The Craft of Fiction,* and E. M. Forster in *Aspects of the Novel,* left it. Mr. Lubbock, writing before *Ulysses,* took us as far as Henry James's "point of view." Mr. Forster, writing after Joyce's Odyssey in Dublin, was still too close to the period when *Ulysses* was either "fantasy" or "a dogged attempt to cover the universe with mud" to understand the full proportions of

8

Joyce's heroic achievement. It was left to Edmund Wilson (in *Axel's Castle*) to show us the symbolist roots of the contemporary novel and to give full weight to the Joycean and Proustian attempt to recreate time past and time present; my debt to him will be readily apparent to readers of this book. I am indebted also to Harry Levin's study of James Joyce, which remains the most penetrating critical estimate we have had of the Irish writer.

My grateful acknowledgments are due to Harold G. Files, professor of English at McGill University in Montreal, who guided my early enthusiasm for the psychological novel; to R. P. Blackmur and E. B. O. Borgerhoff of Princeton University, who invited me to explore my subject at the Christian Gauss Seminar, and to Professor Joseph Prescott of Wayne University whose studies in Joyce have led him to consider the larger problem of the "stream of consciousness" in fiction and who also has been among the very few champions of the work of Dorothy Richardson. And finally I wish to express the deepest gratitude to the members of the two seminars of an inquirer who has been fortunate enough to have active minds against which to launch his ideas and who has been, in turn, admirably challenged to closer definition.

LEON EDEL

9

CONTENTS

11

I

ATMOSPHERE OF THE MIND

On the eve of the First World War three novelists, unknown to each other, were writing works destined to have a remarkable influence on the fiction of our century. In France Marcel Proust, a sickly man and a semi-recluse, deeply introspective and self-absorbed, published in 1913 the first two volumes of the eight-part work we know today as *Remembrance of Things Past*. While these volumes were on the press, an Englishwoman, Dorothy Miller Richardson, vigorously feminist and possessing a considerable awareness of the inner life of her mind, had begun to write what would in the end be a twelve-part novel entitled *Pilgrimage*. The first volume—Miss Richardson called each of the twelve a "chapter"—appeared in 1915, the last in 1938. Between the launching of these two ambitious works on both sides of the Channel, James Joyce, an Irishman, then a teacher of English in the Berlitz school at Trieste, brought out (in 1914) a novel entitled *A Portrait of the Artist as a Young Man*. It was not part of a longer work, like Proust's or Dorothy Richardson's. Yet it was destined to have an important sequel that would mark a turning point in the imaginative literature of our time.

Thus, between 1913 and 1915, was born the modern

psychological novel—what we have come to call, in English letters, the stream-of-consciousness novel or the novel of the silent, the internal monologue, and in French letters, the modern analytic novel which, if not written as *flowing* thought, caught the very atmosphere of the mind.

This was a coincidence indeed—that three writers, unknown to each other, three distinctly different talents and temperaments, should, at the same time, have turned fiction away from external to internal reality, from the outer world that Balzac a century before had charted to the hidden world of fantasy and reverie into which there plays constantly the life and perception of our senses. There were striking similarities in these works, behind their differences. They seemed to be essentially autobiographical. They contained an unusual infusion of the language of poetry. Their very titles suggested, if we include *Ulysses* (which Joyce wrote after the *Portrait*), a curious kinship of search, voyage, pilgrimage. Indeed all were voyages through consciousness. For the three writers were aware, in extraordinary degree, of their feelings and sensations. They were capable, moreover, of candid self-examination, to a degree uncommon even among writers. All three seemed to write from an acute need to cope with inner problems and project their inner life before the world. This may be true of all artists: but in this case the traditional process of projecting the inner experience into an imaginative narrative dealing with the external world was not carried out. These novelists sought to retain and record the "inwardness" of experience.

In the case of Proust, continual illness had fostered the

living and reliving of his novel within the tight walls of a cork-lined room from which he tried to shut out the sound and dust of the world—almost as if the room itself had become his very mind in which thoughts could flow, unmolested by the ruder temperatures and sharper lights of the world outside. As in psycho-analysis the patient is isolated from external stimuli that his mind may play over his past and link it to the present, so Proust in his soundproofed isolation could practice his extraordinary self-analysis. The present assailed him too violently; immediate experience erupted into allergies and the ills of the flesh. In the past there was tranquility—and discovery. By the process of remembering, he found himself.

Experience for Joyce took quite another form. Near-blind from his childhood, he lived in a world of sound, in the ceaseless clamor of the city of his youth, Dublin, which he carried with him whether he was in Trieste, in Zurich or in Paris—and in the end all the cities blended in an ever-increasing din, and their languages mingled, so that Joyce's mind became a Tower of Babel. Unlike Proust, however, Joyce wanted to catch the present, the immediate moment of perception—he called it an "epiphany" applying the religious word to his artist's vision. For Proust, Time Past could become Time Present, to fade immediately into Past again; for Joyce Time Present was all-important—a continuum of Present, in which the Past inevitably lingered.

Miss Richardson seems to have enjoyed better health than her male confreres, although we gather that she too had a sensitivity heightened by myopia. Her work speaks

from a quieter and less dramatic life than that of Proust
or Joyce and it is accordingly more limited. Yet certain
quiet intensities of her inner being clamored to be set
down, and her novel became an experiment to which she
gave all her resources and her devotion. If she was the
least artist of the three, she was an articulate vessel of
feeling, and bent upon challenging the "masculine" novel.
She set out to record the "point of view" of a woman, and
she learned her craft in the process.

Proust began his novel as a direct narrative of memory:

> For a long time I used to go to bed early. Sometimes,
> when I had put out my candle, my eyes would close so
> quickly that I had not even time to say "I'm going to sleep."
> And half an hour later the thought that it was time to go
> to sleep would awaken me; I would try to put away the
> book which, I imagined, was still in my hands, and to blow
> out the light; I had been thinking all the time, while I
> was asleep, of what I had just been reading, but my
> thoughts had run into a channel of their own, until I my-
> self seemed actually to have become the subject of my
> book: a church, a quartet, the rivalry between François I
> and Charles V. . . .

Dorothy Richardson's novel began quite conventionally:

> Miriam left the gaslit hall and went slowly upstairs. The
> March twilight lay upon the landings, but the staircase
> was almost dark. The top landing was quite dark and silent.
> There was no one about. It would be quiet in her room.
> She could sit by the fire and be quiet and think things over
> until Eve and Harriet came back with the parcels. She
> would have time to think about the journey and decide
> what she was going to say to the Fräulein.

Neither of these quiet openings gave any inkling that a major change in the art of fiction was under way. The reader would have to cover several pages before becoming aware that he was on the threshold of innovation: and even then there was some question whether there had been any serious departure from the least rigid of our literary forms—one that embraces works as different as *Tristram Shandy* and *The Ambassadors*. But there was no question of the novelty of James Joyce's opening of *A Portrait of the Artist as a Young Man:*

> Once upon a time and a very good time it was there was a moocow coming down along the road and this moocow that was coming down along the road met a nicens little boy named baby tuckoo . . .
>
> His father told him that story: his father looked at him through a glass: he had a hairy face.
>
> He was baby tuckoo. The moocow came down the road where Betty Byrne lived: she sold lemon platt.
>
> > *O, the wild rose blossoms*
> > *On the little green place.*
>
> He sang that song. That was his song.
>
> > O, the green wothe botheth.
>
> When you wet the bed, first it is warm then it gets cold. His mother put on the oilsheet. That had the queer smell. His mother had a nicer smell than his father. . . .

What the reader discovered, as he read on, was that these were not narratives in the traditional sense. The author (save in the case of Proust) seemed bent on effacing himself and confronting the reader with the direct mental

19

experience of the characters. There were only occasional shifts from past to present, from present to past; what was happening seemed to occur largely at whatever moment the reader happened to be reading the story. This was a distinct departure from the way in which the conventional novels unrolled themselves in majestic leisure with the author constantly telling the story and omniscient to the extent of knowing everything about his characters. This removal of the author from the scene—he remained often an intruder, but was no longer omnipresent—made necessary a significant shift in narrative: it created the need to use the memory of the characters to place the reader into a relationship with their past. There was no "story," no "plot." And above all this kind of novel seemed to turn the reader into an author: it was he, ultimately, who put the story together and he had to keep his wits about him to accumulate his data. The Christmas dinner at the Dedalus household, had it been told by Balzac, would have contained a catalogue of the household furnishings, the menu, and minute descriptions of those at the table. For this Joyce substituted the observations of the boy and the intensities of feeling of the elders: we come to know the Dedalus household not through its physical appearance but through the qualities of feeling that exist within it and their effect on the observant and sensitive Stephen. In *Pointed Roofs*, Miss Richardson gives us our data piecemeal: forty pages must be read before we discover that Miriam's last name is Henderson and we learn that she is seventeen after almost a hundred pages. The reader is enveloped in sensations and daydreams, even as in Proust he remains nearly always with the reminiscential narrator, thinking of all the beds he has slept in and wandering off into the world of Combray, to meet Monsieur Swann, or feel the anguish of the boy awaiting his mother's good-night kiss, and finally to be led to the unrolling of the deliberate, introspective, searching narrative spun like a spider's web from the moment that the madeleine is dipped into the tea. In Joyce, intermittently, one is inside the mind of the developing little boy with his bad eyesight, his acute sense of sound and smell:

> . . . There was the smell of evening in the air, the smell of the fields in the country where they digged up turnips to peel them and eat them when they went out for a walk to Major Barton's, the smell there was in the little woods beyond the pavilion where the gallnuts were.
>
> The fellows were practising long shies and bowling lobs and slow twisters. In the soft grey silence he could hear the bump of the balls: and from here and from there through the quiet air, the sound of the cricket bats: pick, pack, pock, puck: like drops of water in a fountain falling softly in the brimming bowl.

We are nearly always with Stephen: and the *Portrait* of him is a portrait of his sensations and passions, as well as of his thoughts and his intellectual development.

2

This was a new kind of realism, unrelated to the fiction of Arnold Bennett or H. G. Wells or John Galsworthy who had their vogue at the time that these major experiments in psychological fiction were being launched. It was an attempt in a more minute and thorough fashion than ever before to document the whole world of the senses and to catch fugitive thoughts in their progress through the mind —catch them, as Joyce was to do in *Ulysses*—in their very moment of flow. In other words, for the first time, these novelists were seeking to find words that would convey elusive and evanescent thought: not only the words that come to the mind, but the images of the inner world of fantasy, fusing with sounds and smells, the world of perceptual experience. And yet the attempt did not seem new to many critics who pointed out that writers of other centuries, in many countries, had set down the thoughts and reveries of their characters.

What difference, it might be asked, was there between what Joyce attempted and this description of thought in Dostoevsky?

> "It must be the top drawer," he [Raskolnikov] reflected. "So she carries the keys in a pocket on the right. All in one bunch on a steel ring. . . . And there's one key there, three times as big as all the others, with deep notches; that can't be the key of the chest of drawers . . . then there must be some other chest or strong-box . . . that's worth knowing. Strong-boxes always have keys like that . . . but how degrading it all is."

Yet there is a significant difference. It lies in the fact that this is merely unspoken speech and that it is Dostoevsky who tells us "he reflected." In other words, we have here not a flowing stream of thought but a narrator's report— the author being the narrator—of what is occurring in the mind of his character.

22

What then of the soliloquies of Shakespeare? Othello's great debate with himself at the moment when he must act, or Hamlet's

> To die, to sleep;
> To sleep; perchance to dream; ay, there's the rub;
> For in that sleep of death what dreams may come. . . .

But these are *structured* monologues in which the mind presents reasoned and ordered thought, the "end-product" of the stream of consciousness, not the disordered stream itself. A better case might be made for the mad speeches of Lear, yet even these have that "reason in madness" of which Edgar speaks. Still better would be the following, in which Shakespeare attempts to render a chain of associations, flowing from a person into whose mind we are allowed briefly to penetrate. Quoted without the interruptions of other speakers, who on the stage offer a running commentary as the thoughts are revealed, this is what we get:

> Yet here's a spot. Out, damned spot! out, I say! One; two: why, then 'tis time to do't. Hell is murky! Fie, my lord, fie! a soldier and afeard? What need we fear who knows it, when none can call our power to account? Yet who would have thought the old man to have had so much blood in him? The Thane of Fife had a wife: where is she now? What! will these hands n'er be clean? No more o'that, my lord, no more o'that: you mar all with this starting. Here's the smell of blood still: all the perfumes of Araby will not sweeten this little hand. Oh! oh! oh! Wash your hands, put on your night-gown; look not so pale. I tell you yet again, Banquo's buried; he cannot come

out on's grave. To bed, to bed: there's knocking at the gate. Come, come, come, come, give me your hand. What's done cannot be undone. To bed, to bed, to bed.

This is not "stream of consciousness" as we have come to know it in Joyce and Faulkner. It is, nevertheless, closer to it than other examples that have been cited out of the literature of the past. The element of discontinuity is here: there is a seeming mixture of the irrelevant and the relevant—and yet not a word is placed that is not *dramatically* relevant. In this instance, for so Shakespeare had to write it, Lady Macbeth's thoughts coincide with the memories of the audience: they have seen and heard everything that her tortured mind evokes in its somnolent articulateness: they can experience her guilt, her resolution, her courage, her doubt. The impression of a flow of thought is created. And the thoughts flow directly to us from the mind of the personage.

One can find many isolated examples in which writers of the past gave us glimpses into the mind, furtive thoughts, fleeting impressions. Harry Levin has quoted a passage from Fanny Burney's diary which asks "demurely for comparison with the last words of Molly Bloom," but diaries—like letters—tend on the whole to be as structured as soliloquies. Wyndham Lewis, an early critic of the Joycean technique, drew our attention to some of the staccato accents of Alfred Jingle, Esq. in *The Pickwick Papers* and asked us to compare them with those of Leopold Bloom's mind:

Terrible place—dangerous work—other day—five children —mother—tall lady, eating sandwiches—forgot the arch

24

—crash—knock—children look round—mother's head off—
sandwich in her hand—no mouth to put it in—head of a
family off—shocking, shocking. Looking at Whitehall, Sir
—fine place—little window—somebody's else's head off
there, eh, sir?—he didn't keep a sharp look-out enough
either—eh, Sir, eh?

It is quite obvious that one can exhume endless passages
from the literature of the past which resemble the contemporary stream of consciousness or internal monologue.
But to do so is to perhaps dismiss too airily the deeper
meaning for the novel of our time of this "inward-turning"
of a whole group of twentieth century artists.

3

From the first, the novelists of the past were aware that
they could not hope to report to us as circumstantially on
mental data as they could on the physical data of our
world. "These words represent in brief the thousand and
one thoughts which floated through his mind," Balzac
wrote of Eugène de Rastignac, and we have the spectacle
of a great master of fictional detail contenting himself with
a mere digest from the moment he seeks to deal with subjective material. Henry James, at nineteen, when he wrote
an anonymously-published story, was precociously careful
to distinguish between action which he could describe with
Defoesque verisimilitude, and thoughts which belonged to
someone else—and which the author, theoretically, could
not adequately possess:

Though I have judged best, hitherto, often from an exag-
gerated fear of trenching on the ground of fiction, to tell

you what this poor lady did and said, rather than what she thought, I may disclose what passed in her mind now.

Dostoevsky, in one of his tales, stated the problem implied in Balzac's sentence with the utmost clarity:

It is well known that whole trains of thought sometimes pass through our brains instantaneously, as though they were sensations, without being translated into human speech, still less into a literary language. But we will try to translate these sensations of our hero's, and present to the reader at least the kernel of them, so to say, what was most essential and nearest to reality in them. For many of our sensations when translated into ordinary language seem absolutely unreal. That is why they never find expression, though everyone has them.

The novelists of the nineteenth century thus agreed that subjective states could be *reported* but not *rendered* in the novel. And William James's brilliant account of the psychology of thought in his *Principles of Psychology* of 1890 offered a striking confirmation of this view. It was William James who named the "stream of consciousness"; the metaphor was invoked by him to describe the flux of the mind, its continuity and yet its continuous change.

Consciousness, William James said, is an amalgam of all that we have experienced and continue to experience. Every thought is a part of a personal consciousness; every thought is also unique and ever-changing. We seem to be selective in our thoughts, selectively attentive or inattentive, focusing attention on certain objects and areas of experience, rejecting others, totally blocking others out. When a thought recurs in the mind it can never be exactly the same as it was before. Renewed, it carries with it the freshness of renewal, and the new context in which it has re-emerged. "Experience is remoulding us every moment, and our mental reaction on every given thing is really a resultant of our experience of the whole world up to that date." This is true of course not only for ideas, but for our sensory perceptions as the consciousness registers them.

Thought has changes of pace. It involves a "clearly lighted center of experience" surrounded by a twilight region—a "fringe" or "halo" of other thoughts. What is important for us above all, however, is William James's description of the difficulty of catching the thoughts in their flow, of arresting them and examining them.

> The rush of thought is so headlong that it almost always brings us up at the conclusion before we can arrest it. Or if our purpose is nimble enough and we do arrest it, it ceases forthwith to be itself. As a snowflake crystal caught in the warm hand is no longer a crystal but a drop, so, instead of catching the feeling of relation moving to its term, we find we have caught some substantive thing, usually the last word we were pronouncing, statically taken, and with its function, tendency, and particular meaning in the sentence quite evaporated. The attempt at introspective analysis in these cases is in fact like seizing a spinning top to catch its motion, or trying to turn up the gas quickly enough to see how the darkness looks.

Does this mean that the novelist, in seeking to write of what goes on in the mind, attempts the impossible? Is he foredoomed to continual frustration in his attempt to put consciousness into words, to find always there is light instead of darkness when he seeks to turn his light upon the darkness, or that the snowdrop turns to water even as he holds it in his hand? Is there no way in which to seize the spinning top and to keep it spinning at the same time?

How render in prose fiction our immediate perception of the world around us, the multitude of direct impressions and the "fringes" and "haloes" of thought, conscious and unconscious, that surround them while, say, we are delivering a reasonably straight sentence to a friend seated opposite us at a table? We may note the details of his face as we talk, its expression, its coloring, or the color of his attire, or the shape of his necktie, or the wart on his neck; the distinctive aspects may float into the clearly lighted center of our experience or remain on the fringe, while we are aware of thinking about what we are saying and at the same time an active fantasy is playing through our mind on still another level that may reflect the feelings we have about the person opposite us, or may wander away entirely from the scene to field and sea, or other faces, or a game of golf, even while we still coherently address the man and even while our eyes catch his expression and register it and our ears record his laughter, his words, the noise of a passing car, a distant train whistle, the clatter of dishes, the girl three tables away putting on lipstick; and at the same time we raise automatically the cup of coffee to our lips, aware of its taste (even to noting the components, say, the amount of sugar we have put in), and its temperature, and if we are inclined to Proustian association, the sip may evoke other coffee-drinkings that in turn flood our memory as if it were a flickering cinema that pulls together images and words; and through all this the talk is sustained and the figure opposite is unaware of the richness of our multitudinous impressions—as we are unaware of its impressions, save those it will articulate.

This quite structured attempt on my part to indicate the simultaneity of mental experience can only be a skeleton-diagram of consciousness. It cannot begin to convey the complexity of thought and of sensory experience. How record, word by word, such symphonic material, in which certain instruments often speak out but in which, around them, the voices of others are constantly breaking in? How keep the core of thought disengaged from the haloes and fringes? It cannot be done, and if it could it would tax our reading attention far beyond its capacity. The result, in any event, would be of as dubious artistic value as a gramophone record of the noises in the restaurant.

We recognize, therefore, that Balzac and Dostoevsky were right when they spoke of the need to digest the thoughts of their characters and of *translating* sensations into words. What they could not have taken into account at that time was the possibility of the artist's creating the *illusion* that we are inside the mind of the character by the same process that, say Balzac, creates the illusion that we are inside the Maison Vauquer: by the massing of detail in such a way that the interior comes alive, so that we feel ourselves within the boarding house and among its people as the story unfolds. Or, what the nineteenth century writers could not foresee, that an interior such as the Dedalus home at Christmas, could be re-created not by the massing of the realistic physical detail, but by making real for us the intense emotions within that household. The critics, in the 1920's took a wrong turning (later amply rectified), when they said that James Joyce had not accurately given us the thoughts of his characters in *Ulysses*. They spoke as if Joyce had turned a motion-picture camera into the minds of Stephen and Leopold and Molly and was supposed to convey to us everything that it found there. Even so thoughtful a practitioner of the craft of fiction as Edith Wharton described stream-of-consciousness writing as the recording of the "unsorted abundance" of thought and impression. These critics failed to understand that Joyce was exercising close selection and arrangement even when he seemed to dredge up a great deal of unrelated associational matter. His selection was addressed to the creating of an illusion *that there had been no selection.* For Joyce was aware that his was an act of *translating* into words material that by its evanescence, defied verbal description. He knew, in other words, the lessons of the symbolist movement.

4

We return to old ground, we are back among the symbolists and their revolt against naturalism. We are also back in the 1880's, again listening to the famous debate on the novel between Sir Walter Besant and Henry James with Robert Louis Stevenson eloquently chiming in. It was Stevenson who joined the issue with great clarity:

Life is monstrous, infinite, illogical, abrupt and poignant; a work of art, in comparison, is neat, finite, self-contained, rational, flowing and emasculate. Life imposes by brute energy, like inarticulate thunder; art catches the ear among the far louder noises of experience like an air artificially made by a discreet musician. . . . The novel which is a work of art exists, not by its resemblances to life, which are forced and material, as a shoe must still consist of leather, but by its immeasurable difference from life, which is designed and significant, and is both the method and the meaning of the work.

Substitute the word "thought" or "perceptual experience" for "life" in this striking passage, and Stevenson's remarks would apply with equal force to the novel of subjectivity.

In this same debate, Henry James extended the definition of experience and the province of fiction to include the subjective world:

Humanity is immense and reality has a myriad forms; the most one can affirm is that some of the flowers of fiction have the odour of it, and others have not; as for telling you in advance how your nosegay should be composed, that is another affair. It is equally excellent and inconclusive to say that one must write from experience; to our supposititious aspirant such a declaration might savour of mockery. What kind of experience is intended, and where does it begin and end? Experience is never limited, and it is never complete; it is an immense sensibility, a kind of huge spider-web of the finest silken threads suspended in the chamber of consciousness, and catching every airborne particle in its tissue. It is the very atmosphere of the mind; and when the mind is imaginative—much more when it happens to be that of a man of genius—it takes to itself the faintest hints of life, it converts the very pulses of the air into revelations.

Atmosphere of the mind. This is a very happy phrase. It comes closer to describing—insofar as it is describable—what the writers of novels dealing with the subjective life of their characters have tried to do. Whether they seek to render mental experience through one or another of the techniques that have been devised—and the writers have been extremely inventive in discovering new ones—or resort simply to the first person self-analysis of Proust, they are invariably trying to capture for the reader the atmosphere of the mind.

From the moment they do so, certain important problems arise involving the relationship between the writer and his characters and the writer and the reader. For the writer there is the initial problem of the *kind* of mind he will select. It is obvious that the duller the mind, the more resourceful he will have to be in maintaining the interest of the reader. Once he has made this choice he must face a second problem: the writer must in some way disengage himself from his character. The thoughts, whether stream of consciousness or internal monologue, must speak for themselves without his intervening as narrator. This is not as new a problem as it might seem. "The artist ought to be in his work like God in creation, invisible and all-powerful; let him be felt everywhere but not seen," wrote Flaubert long ago. Taine's image was that of the artist cutting the umbilical that bound him to his work. Joyce, facing this problem in writing his subjective fiction, was echoing Flaubert when he described the dramatic artist as one who "like the God of the creation, remains within or behind or beyond or above his handiwork . . . paring his fingernails." And this raises the further question—it will deserve a whole chapter to itself—whether an artist drawing upon the contents of his own mind (which is the only mind he can use in his creation), is really able to detach himself from his characters: that is whether their subjectivity is not, in reality, *his* subjectivity. In other words: is not a subjective novel but a disguised form of autobiography? To this Proust offers us a definitive answer, as we shall see.

Difficult as these problems are, there remains perhaps the most difficult of all. Once the attempt is made to render a certain mind, there ensues the meeting of that mind with the mind of the reader. There can follow a merging of the two mental atmospheres. In the old novels this was not the case. The reader was being told a story. He listened. He was drawn into it primarily through identification with one or another of the characters. In the modern psychological novel there is no "story" in the old sense, and there is only one character (at a time) with which to identify. If the author succeeds in drawing the reader into this single consciousness, he should be able to make the reader *feel* with the character: and the reader does this only if proper identification with the character is achieved. He then may hear the same sounds of Dublin Bloom hears, or feel the sea-shells crunching underfoot as he walks not only with but *as* Dedalus on the beach; or pause to hear the bronze tones of Big Ben as Mrs. Dalloway, or allow his own smell-memory to come into play when Benjy, in *The Sound and the Fury*, tells him that Caddy smelled like trees or that Versh smelled like rain. The entire Benjy section reads like the opening paragraphs of *A Portrait of the Artist as a Young Man*. We are in the mind here, however, of a mentally retarded individual who has been "'three years old thirty years.'" And it is Faulkner's achievement to have made Benjy real for us even when we cannot wholly identify with him, since he makes us aware of the poetry of the idiot mind, provoking in us compassion and sympathy. He has at the same time maneuvered us into the double position of reading on Benjy's childish level of awareness—as a direct experience—while exercising our own adult capacities to make sense out of the data furnished by Benjy's mind. There is, in other words, the story that is told by the flowing thoughts of Benjy—and the story to be deduced from them by the reader.

What is remarkable about a novel such as *Ulysses,* or the Faulkner novel of which we have been speaking, is that by the time we have finished reading it we have visited —indeed we have lived—inside the minds of several persons. This we cannot do in our everyday life, where we are shut up in only one consciousness—our own. By this process of involving us directly in the mental experience of the characters, the psychological novel has added a significant dimension to the art of prose fiction. To read such a novel can be as never before an enlargement of our own experience. The old-time reader of novels sat down with his book and made a simple demand upon the author: "Beguile me, offer me comedy and tears, tell me about droll people and lovers, and a story that will keep me rooted to the spot and my eyes glued to the page." The case is reversed when we come to the subjective novel. It is the author who says to the reader: "Here is the artistic record of a mind, at the very moment that it is thinking. Try to penetrate within it. You will know only as much as this mind may reveal. It is you, not I, who will piece together any 'story' there may be. Of course I have arranged this illusion for you. But it is you who must experience it."

II

THE INWARD TURNING

It was in reality no coincidence that Marcel Proust, James Joyce and Dorothy Richardson found themselves writing psychological novels at the century's turn. They were children of the romantic century: rationalism and reason had long before yielded to introspection and feeling. If classicism was intellect and repose, romanticism was self-absorption and flux. The romantic hero began by contemplating his heart; he ended by contemplating his mind. And he discovered that heart, symbol of feeling and perception, and mind, symbol of thought and reason, could be closely related. Often the mind tried to explain away that which the heart felt.

The psychological novel, accidentally founded by Samuel Richardson, by the use of an epistolary method that brought the reader close to the thoughts and feelings of his characters, had given way to the self-conscious modern psychological novel, in which the thoughts and feelings themselves were re-created. Coleridge described Samuel Richardson as recording "the morbid consciousness of every thought and feeling in the whole flux and reflux of the mind, in short its self-involution and dream-like continuity." Criticism is never more fertile than when, in assessing the past, it sees into the future. Coleridge, in writing of "the flux and reflux of the mind" in reality was describing what the stream-of-consciousness novel would attempt to do. It was he who spoke also of the "twilight reaches of consciousness" and the "modes of inmost being" in describing the "willing suspension of disbelief" which every writer asks of his reader. Maupassant expressed the same thought when he wrote: *Faire vrai consiste . . . à donner l'illusion complète du vrai . . . les Réalistes de talent devraient s'appeler plutôt des Illusionists*. And Baudelaire spoke of "suggestive magic" as being the function of "pure art," which Jules Laforgue re-expressed when he wrote that "the work of art can never be the equivalent of fugitive reality." If the symbolists, and the naturalists against whom they revolted, regarded themselves as irreconcilable, the two had, at bottom, similar ends in view. The naturalist might cling to his weighty documents and the symbolist to his symbols: both, however, wanted to create an *illusion* of reality.

The modern psychological novel is "modern" in that it reflects the deeper and more searching *inwardness* of our century, and this turning inward was reflected in the writings of William James and Henri Bergson and after them, on the experimental and clinical level, in the work of Sigmund Freud. Their exploration of the psychology of thought—of consciousness—went far beyond the mere analysis of it such as Hume and Locke, Berkeley and Mill had courageously attempted. When Proust, Joyce and Dorothy Richardson began to write, the influence of Freud was only beginning to be felt; and it is to Bergson, in his influence on Proust (and to some extent on Joyce), and to William James, in his account of thought-experience, that we must look as the creators of the intellectual atmosphere in which the novel of subjectivity came into being. As has often been the case, changes in philosophical thought heralded technical innovations in the arts.

We know that Proust studied briefly under Bergson and that he read his works. He mentions him only once, in *Cities of the Plain* (*Sodome et Gomorrhe*) in connection with the effects of soporific drugs on memory. Memory, however, is at the heart of Bergson's explorations, as it is of Proust's. Bergson's concept of time—*la durée*—as the measure of existence, "the invisible progress of the past, which gnaws into the future," his thesis of the use of the past in the evolution of the creative act, his discussions of intuition and reality, his belief in the flux of experience—all of these ideas are taken up and studied with extraordinary refinement by Proust. Like William James, Bergson taught that we are remoulded constantly by experience; that consciousness is a process of endless accretion, so long as mind and senses are functioning; that it is "the continuation of an indefinite past in a living present." And out of this comes also the preoccupation with time which is central to the psychological novel. The watch measures off the hours with continuing regularity, but consciousness sometimes makes an hour seem like a day or a day like an hour. In the mind past and present merge: we suddenly call up a memory of childhood that is chronologically of the distant past; but in it memory becomes instantly vivid and is re-lived for the moment that it is recalled. So, in setting down in the novel the thoughts as they are passing through the mind of the character, the novelist is catching and recording the present moment—and no other. It was no accident that Joyce sought to record a single day in *Ulysses* and that throughout Virginia Woolf there is a preoccupation with "the moment."

It would be wrong, however, to attach Proust solely to Bergson. In Bergson he found certain important—and congenial—philosophical and psychological ideas; to give them expression, artistically, he turned to the literary movement that was at its height when he came to maturity. For Proust had learned much from the symbolists; and what they believed—on an artistic level—came very close to Bergsonism. Bergson described the flux of life. They sought to frame it in words. The evanescence of experience, they held, could be evoked in literature only through the use of images and symbols—the personal symbols of a given artist. It required the verbal beauty of the mind to express the mind. "My keyboard is perpetually changing," wrote Laforgue, "and there is no other keyboard which is identical with mine." The roots of Proust's novel reach deeply into the symbolist movement.

What of Joyce?

In as complex a figure, nourished on Aquinas and on Vico, aware of the literary movements of his time and able to draw upon many literatures by virtue of his great linguistic gifts, we must expect to find a meeting of many sources. These have been described and dealt with in great detail by the many critics of the Irish writer and doubtless much remains to be explored. But there is one source which primarily concerns us in the present inquiry. It was widely proclaimed by Joyce himself, yet it has not been taken seriously enough. In his twentieth year, James Joyce read a French novel of 1888—written at the height of the symbolist ferment. It was by Édouard Dujardin and was titled *Les lauriers sont coupés*. George Moore had talked about it in Dublin and about its author, who was his friend. Joyce appears to have been profoundly impressed by its narrative technique. From the first word to the last, the reader found himself inside the mind of the principal character. Very little actually happens in the book. A young man-about-town in Paris is in love with an actress. She asks him constantly for money; this he gives to her in the hope that ultimately she will bestow upon him more than sweet words and a smile. His hopes turn out to be ill founded. It is, as fiction, a pretty small affair. One would hardly think it capable of influencing, even in remote fashion, so largely-proportioned a work as *Ulysses*. Yet Joyce, when asked where his stream-of-consciousness technique stemmed from, always announced his debt to Édouard Dujardin. Dujardin was then still alive, although his novel had been long forgotten. The French writer promptly likened himself to Lazarus rising from the dead—and indeed he was a living author who had gained a glimpse of his posthumous reputation. Joyce proclaimed his debt to Dujardin, Dujardin proclaimed *his* debt to Joyce. The present had exalted the past. *Les lauriers sont coupés* was reprinted with a Preface by Valéry Larbaud, the French critic who first explained the Homeric structure of *Ulysses*. The book was reviewed as if it were a new work, and its method of narration was baptized *post factum* by Larbaud as *le monologue intérieur*. In a lecture delivered in 1930, Dujardin sought to define internal monologue and attributed to Paul Bourget the first use of the term. While it is interesting to think of Bourget, with his passion for what passed as "psychology" in his time, as the originator of the term, the credit for its application to the subjective or stream-of-consciousness novel really belongs to Larbaud.

Mary Colum, in her reminiscences, claims that Joyce's resuscitation of the Dujardin novel was a hoax, an elaborately embroidered Joycean joke. If she is right it was a cruel joke perpetrated upon an elderly and much-respected man of letters—and one taken much too seriously by the literary world to be funny. A reading of the Dujardin novel, however, supplies the answer and can set our mind at rest. Faded and distant it is, but it is without a doubt the first consistently-sustained (even though technically-primitive) stream-of consciousness novel to have been written.

It is easy to see how Joyce could have pondered upon Dujardin's experiment, taken stock of its errors, and built upon it with the extraordinary verbal skill which he possessed and which made it possible for him to succeed where Dujardin failed. In acknowledging his debt to Dujardin Joyce was, by implication, acknowledging his debt to the symbolist movement, for Dujardin was of the symbolists, and his work sprang directly from the Tuesdays at Mallarmé's and the literary ferment in the Paris of the 1880's.

Edmund Wilson long ago defined the relationship between the symbolists and the work of Joyce and Proust, in his admirable study, *Axel's Castle.* In that volume he distilled from the elaborate theorizing of the French poets the essence of symbolist doctrine as follows:

> Every feeling or sensation we have, every moment of consciousness, is different from every other; and it is, in consequence, impossible to render our sensations as we actually experience them through the conventional and universal language of ordinary literature. Each poet has his unique personality; each of his moments has its special tone, its special combination of elements. And it is the poet's task to find, to invent, the special language which will alone be capable of expressing his personality and feelings. . . .

This, in effect, is what the symbolists sought to do and in Joyce there was to be the strange and rewarding—and paradoxical—spectacle of a supreme realist, in the tradition of both Flaubert and Zola, turning to the methods of the symbolists to achieve his realism. When it was published, the Dujardin novel (as might be expected) attracted very little attention. However Rémy de Gourmont's critical eye caught it and he described it as "a novel which seems in literature a transposed anticipation of the cinema." George Moore, who corresponded with Dujardin, read the book during its serialization in *La Revue Indépendante* and wrote to him that it revealed for the first time "the inner life of the soul." He added *"seulement je crains la monotonie. Nous verrons; en tout cas, c'est neuf."* Moore's fears that the method might prove monotonous pointed to one of its possible shortcomings. That, however, remained to be discovered.

2

If Proust and Joyce stemmed from the enveloping climate of introspection and subjectivity—in reality the continued flowering of romanticism—in the late nineteenth century, with certain significant points of attachment to the symbolists, what impulse set Dorothy Richardson on her elaborate fictional experiment? Readers who asked this question found no direct answer. There was no doubt that if Miss Richardson's succeeding volumes did appear to reach a dead level of monotony for some, she was nevertheless faithfully adhering to her method. By the time the eighth volume—or chapter—had appeared, in 1925 (*The Trap*), readers knew little more about the "hard" facts of Miriam Henderson's life than they had discovered in the first volume. They knew, however, a great deal about her moods and her feelings and the quality of her mind; and they remained sealed in the envelope of her consciousness. Quite the most remarkable part of Miss Richardson's experiment was her unswerving adherence to the *single* point of view. *The Trap,* however, yielded a highly significant bit of information.

In this portion of *Pilgrimage,* Miriam Henderson is moving into a new apartment. Very early we come upon allusions to a book which has made a profound impression upon the heroine. But she never names it.

> Her forgotten book was lying on the table. The book that
> had suddenly become the centre of her life. . . . She took
> it in her hands, felt it draw her again with its unique power.

The movers arrive to take her things to the new apartment. She, however, is absorbed by the book.

> The men could, must, manage without supervision. For the second time, during which they stood listening as though she had not spoken before, she pointed out the things which were to be taken, and sat down with the book.

She surveys the volume and its letters of gold on a red cover, and remembers how she found it in the subscription library among rows of well-known names of books and writers. (It is a defect in the internal monologue that the title of the book and the name of its author do not once enter the mind of the heroine: and this is difficult to believe, for she fondles the volume and thinks much about it.)

> And then this book, for all the neutrality of its title and of the author's name, drawing her hands, bringing, as she took it from the shelf and carried it, unexamined, away down the street, the stillness of contentment.
>
> She could, so long as the men remained, get no further. Within the neat red binding lay the altogether new happiness. . . .

There follow more details of the moving and then we return to the volume:

> She glanced through the pages of its opening chapter, the chapter that was now part of her own experience; set down at last alive, so that the few pages stood in her mind, growing as a single good day will grow, in memory, deep and wide, wider than the year to which it belongs. She was surprised to find, coming back after the interval of disturbed days, how little she had read. Just the open-

ing pages, again and again, not wanting to go forward; wanting the presentation of the two men, talking outside time and space in the hotel bedroom, to go on for ever. And presently fearing to read further, lest the perfection of satisfaction should cease.

The identity of the book becomes a charming puzzle for the reader and there is a kind of teasing perversity in the way in which Miss Richardson feeds us the data: neutral title, neutral name of author, two men talking "outside time and space" in a hotel bedroom. We read on wondering whether we are to be totally frustrated. For in Miss Richardson's novel certain thoughts trickle through Miriam's consciousness never to be explained, never to return—as happens in all minds. There is a remark on the second page of the first volume, "Perhaps Miss Gilkes was right . . ." but we never discover who Miss Gilkes was. Would Miriam reveal the name of this book which she deemed to be so important, or the name of its author? And then:

> Reading a paragraph here and there, looking out once more the two phrases that had thrilled her more intimately than any others, she found a stirring of strange statements in her mind. A strange clarity that was threatening to change the adventure of reading to a shared disaster. For she remembered now, having hung for a while over Waymarsh's "sombre glow". . . .

There at last we have it! Waymarsh and Strether in the hotel at Chester. Miriam has in her hands, in the Methuen edition, the red cover with the title stamped in gold, *The Ambassadors,* by Henry James.

This man was a monstrous unilluminated pride. And joy in him was a mark of the same corruption. Pride in discovering the secrets of his technique. Pride in watching it labour with the development of the story. The deep attention demanded by this new way of statement was in itself a self-indulgence. . . . But the cold ignorance of this man was unconscious. And therefore innocent. And it was he after all who had achieved the first completely satisfying way of writing a novel. If this were a novel.

The first completely satisfying way of writing a novel . . . This new way of statement. . . . What had Dorothy Richardson discovered in Henry James that seemed so important to her—or rather to her heroine—so important indeed as to be now "the centre of her life?" The question is worth pursuing.

III

THE POINT OF VIEW

WHAT DID DOROTHY RICHARDSON MEAN WHEN SHE SPOKE OF "the first completely satisfying way of writing a novel," as she placed a copy of *The Ambassadors* in the hands of Miriam Henderson? From the few clues she gives us, she seems to have read only as far as Lambert Strether's dinner in London with Maria Gostrey. Yet she discerns in the book, in its first half a hundred pages, some quality or technique that seems to her—some time before 1910—a "new way of statement."

This new way of statement was Henry James's predilection for maintaining a consistent viewpoint or level of awareness through which the reader is given the facts of his story. He is very careful to explain in the Preface to *The Ambassadors,* written for the New York Edition of his works (not the red-covered first edition read by Miriam), how he has handled his narrative. He might have written a first person story; but "the first person, in the long piece, is a form foredoomed to looseness." Looseness, he adds, "was never much my affair." His readers, I think, will agree.

What then did he do? Instead of allowing his hero, Strether, to reveal himself, his age, his past, his special mission in Europe, (as he would in the first person) James sets his ironic comedy into motion in the hotel at Chester: he establishes a play of illumination among three persons. First, Strether, arriving and thinking briefly of the errand that has brought him to Europe, but having no occasion to disclose it; then the chance encounter with Maria Gostrey, who has known Waymarsh and hears Strether speak of him; and finally Waymarsh's arrival. There follows the scene in the hotel room in which Waymarsh attempts to discover from Strether the nature of his special "mission" in Europe, although Strether is clearly in no hurry to talk about it. Finally the three characters arrive in London after sundry minor adventures of sightseeing and shopping. All the while Strether is receiving impressions and developing more and more a sense of release from the responsibilities and constraints of Woollett, Massachusetts, and Mrs. Newsome who has sent him abroad as her "ambassador."

The "new way of statement" is through a kind of mutual irradiation—Strether illuminating Maria, she illuminating him, both illuminating Waymarsh, and Waymarsh in turn holding up his lamp to look at the other two. It is the method of the drama, the unraveling of an exposition as we get it on the stage, but with the much greater subtlety which a novel permits. Gradually the novel will shift into the mind of Strether, and it is his mind that will light up the whole revelation of Paris and of his task—the initial purpose of which was to rescue Chad Newsome from what Woollett believed was the arms of a French temptress. Quietly James will hand the kite string of his story to the reader.

This is what Dorothy Richardson perceived at the time of the novel's publication—and it was perception enough in those days when Henry James's public greeted his books with ever-increasing bewilderment.

2

James called this particular method of revelation of the story, that is illumination of the situation and characters through one or several minds, the *point of view.* Very early in his career he had discovered the trick of making the characters reveal themselves with minimal intervention of the author. But it was not until the writing of his final Prefaces that he fully explained the theories that had guided him. In the very first Preface, discussing the character of Rowland Mallet, in *Roderick Hudson,* he tells us that the "centre of interest throughout *Roderick* is in Rowland Mallet's consciousness, and the drama is the very drama of that consciousness." He goes on to explain that he had to make this consciousness acute but "not *too* acute" for that would have made it superhuman. In other words "the beautiful little problem was to keep it connected, connected intimately, with the general human exposure, and thereby bedimmed and befooled and bewildered, anxious, restless, fallible, and yet to endow it with such intelligence that the appearances reflected in it, and constituting together there the situation and the 'story,' should become by that fact intelligible." This was the key to the Jamesian method; and Rowland's step-by-step discoveries of the situation before him, and his relation to it, provide an unfolding drama.

In the Preface to *The Portrait of a Lady*—a work he deemed "the most proportioned" of his fictions after *The Ambassadors*—he dwells on what he considered the great scene of that novel, his heroine's review, late one night, of the course her life had taken.

> She sits up, by her dying fire, far into the night, under the spell of recognitions on which she finds the last sharpness suddenly wait. It is a representation simply of her motion-lessly *seeing*, and an attempt withal to make the mere still lucidity of her act as "interesting" as the surprise of a cara-van or the identification of a pirate. It represents, for that matter, one of the identifications dear to the novelist, and even indispensable to him; but it all goes on without her being approached by another person and without her leav-ing her chair. It is obviously the best thing in the book, but it is only a supreme illustration of the general plan.

The "general plan" in James was to make the reflections of an individual as exciting as an adventure story. James states the plan as if it were a recipe: "Place the centre of the subject in the young woman's own consciousness and you get as interesting and as beautiful a difficulty as you could wish. Stick to *that*—for the centre; put the heaviest weight into *that* scale, which will be so largely the scale of her relation to herself. Make her only interested enough, at the same time, in the things that are not herself, and this relation needn't fear to be too limited. Place meanwhile in the other scale the lighter weight . . . press least hard, in short, on the consciousness of your heroine's satellites, especially the male; make it an interest contributive only to the greater one." James mused that by this means he

could produce the "maximum of intensity with the mini-
mum of strain." Isabel's vigil and meditation—it is, in
effect, a scrupulously-organized and highly-sifted internal
monologue—is for James a "vigil of searching criticism."
The point of view is at the center of James's esthetic of the
novel. And it must be at the center of any study of the
stream of consciousness in the contemporary novel: for
once we are within a given mind we can obviously have
only the inner vision, the *point of view* of that particular
mind. In studying the problems of his fixed and varying
centers of consciousness, Henry James was preparing the
way for those who would follow and carry this technique
to its logical conclusion: to record the action of the mind
itself.

3

There are, on the long Jamesian shelf, two pieces of
fiction which admirably illustrate the novelist's cunning
experiments with the point of view. One of them, *The Turn
of the Screw*, has become the subject of a long and rather
tiresome controversy arising from a discussion of the circumstantial evidence in the narrative, with the participants, however, failing to examine the technique of the
story-telling, which would have made much of the dispute
unnecessary. The second has met with general critical
bafflement. I refer to *The Sacred Fount*, written in 1900,
just before *The Ambassadors*. Two critics R. P. Blackmur
and Edward Sackville-West, have recognized the qualities
of art in this short novel, without, however, looking closely
at its structure; Edmund Wilson, on the other hand, has

understood the structure but has described the novel as "mystifying, even maddening" thereby paying perhaps unintended tribute to Henry James's conscious attempt at "mystification." Other critics, and they are numerous, have either masked their bewilderment in derision or candidly admitted they could not understand. William Dean Howells achieved a rather curious position between the two extremes: he announced, when the book was published, he had mastered its secret, but said he had decided he "wouldn't for the present divulge it." "For the present" lasted seventeen years; thereafter Howells was beyond divulging. Perhaps the most quoted verdict on this novel has been Rebecca West's: that it is "a small, mean story," and that it "worries one like a rat nibbling at the wainscot," a story of how "a week-end visitor spends more intellectual force than Kant can have used on *The Critique of Pure Reason,* in an unsuccessful attempt to discover whether there exists between certain of his fellow-guests a relationship not more interesting among these vacuous people than it is among sparrows."

When criticism throws up its hands in bewilderment over the work of an artist or wavers between such extremes, it is reasonable to inquire whether the work in question is really art. Has there been a failure in communication or a failure in perception—or both? For us the question is pertinent, since in both these works James came closest to creating that type of bewilderment which contemporary novel readers feel at first, say, when they open *The Sound and the Fury* and are plunged into the shifting conscious-

ness of Benjy. Dostoevsky had preceded James in a remarkable story, *Notes from the Underground* but there,
in the first paragraph, he had semaphored the reader, not
with flags but with klieg lights that here was the mind of
an eccentric, if not a madman. There is no such obvious
signaling in *The Turn of the Screw* or *The Sacred Fount.*
In both of these works the reader is led unsuspectingly to
accept the narrator in good faith, and this may have been
what James meant when he said he had set "a trap for
the unwary." In *The Turn of the Screw,* James even provides an elaborate testimonial to the good character of the
unnamed governess, who is the first-person narrator. Yet
in both cases, if the reader reads attentively, he will discover that he is tied down by the limitations James imposes
upon him. The data given goes only so far: beyond, he can
have recourse only to his own imagination.

There are, so to speak, three narrators in *The Turn of
the Screw.* The first is the individual, perhaps James
himself, who begins by telling us "The story had held us,
round the fire. . . ." This unidentified First Narrator goes
on to mention a second personage named Douglas. Douglas now briefly takes over the narrative; he tells of a ghost
story with a special "turn of the screw." It is related in an
old manuscript. Douglas is thus, in a certain sense, a Second Narrator, but not technically, since his account is at
first being quoted or summarized by the First Narrator.
Then, finally, Douglas begins to read the manuscript and
the Principal Narrator, the governess, takes over. The
story we finally are given is hers, and it is told in the first

person. Douglas and the First Narrator disappear never to return.

Readers often become so wrapped up in the ghosts and the children of *The Turn of the Screw* that they forget this elaborate setting. In it a great deal of significant information is given to us. Each narrator provides a set of facts, not, however, evaluated for us. We are told the governess has been dead for twenty years. She sent the manuscript to Douglas before she died. Douglas tells us she was ten years older than he was and that she was his sister's governess. "She struck me as awfully clever and nice. . . . I liked her extremely." She was twenty when the events described in the manuscript occurred. We are told that forty years have elapsed since her death. Douglas says "it was long ago" that he knew her and "this episode was long before." In fact he was at Trinity College "and I found her at home on my coming down the second summer." This means that Douglas must have been eighteen or perhaps twenty when he had completed his second year at the university; and the governess, ten years older, would be about thirty when Douglas met her and found her "nice." And the meeting was ten years after the events described in her manuscript.

This is an elaborate and careful time-scheme for James to have set down and he did so not merely through whim. We know from his working notebooks the care with which he placed every detail in his fictions. The time-scheme is extremely important in this story. It establishes, for one thing, that Douglas's testimony is based on the personality of the governess as it was ten years *after* the events of the story. By that time we can presume she had learned the ways of the world. We are explicitly told that at twenty she knew little of the world; she had emerged from a cloistered Hampshire vicarage, the youngest of several daughters of a poor and—as she describes him—eccentric country parson. The narrative itself emphasizes her rusticity and unworldliness: she had never seen herself in a full-length mirror; she had never read a novel (and at Bly she reads Fielding's *Amelia* which has the word "rape" and the word "adultery" on its first page); she has never seen a play. If we add to these little details the significant fact that she has received her position from a mysterious and handsome gentleman in Harley Street who sends her to Bly to take care of his nephew and niece with only a maid and an ignorant but well-meaning housekeeper (her name, Mrs. Grose, suggests the quality of her mind), for company, it becomes clear that she has ample reason to be nervous about the duties and responsibilities conferred on her. Moreover she is given *carte blanche*: she must make her own decisions and may not communicate with her employer. These are circumstances enough to make for nervousness and anxiety in a young girl taking her first job. In effect she has jumped from a humble parsonage to the role of mistress of a country house and to vicarious motherhood of two beautiful children.

What happens thereafter, by her own account, is a story of her throbbing sense of insecurity and her unbridled speculations about the governess who preceded her and the valet with whom that governess was friendly—both of whom are dead. Her daydreams are filled with the figure

61

of the man in Harley Street; she takes evening walks hoping to meet him. She encounters instead her first vision of Peter Quint. He is on the tower; he wears the clothes of the man in Harley Street; she sees him only from the waist up.

The governess's account of her stay at Bly is riddled with inconsistencies which the many critics who have discussed the story have never sufficiently perceived. There are moments when she is, in a less mad way, doing what the retired civil servant does in Dostoevsky's *Notes from the Underground*. She speculates and she assumes—and what she first states as fancy she later states as fact. Most readers have tended to accept her story as "fact" partly because Douglas has given her such a good character at the outset and particularly because of the cunning which James has employed in telling the story.

Let us glance at the second occasion on which the governess sees Quint, that is on the day he appears looking through the window of the dining room. She does not know that it is Quint, or that he is a ghost. She sees him again from the waist up.

> On the spot there came to me the added shock of a certitude that it was not for me he had come there. He had come for someone else.
>
> The flash of this knowledge—for it was knowledge in the midst of dread—produced in me the most extraordinary effect, started, as I stood there, a sudden vibration of duty and courage.

We must remember that we are receiving from the governess her story and *her* interpretation of what she saw or imagined. We are entirely in her mind. She had seen a strange man and she does not at this moment know that he is anything but a palpable man; he resembles the man seen on the tower. But she has the "shock of certitude" that "it was not for me he had come there." He had come for "someone else." This is to say the least an assumption. But the governess promptly appropriates it as "knowledge in the midst of dread." It is "certitude."

There follows the first vision of the woman, Miss Jessel, or a person the governess believes to be Miss Jessel. She is seen by the governess, or rather *felt*, on the other side of the pond which they have named, in Flora's geography lesson, the Sea of Azof.

> . . . I became aware that, on the other side of the Sea of Azof, we had an interested spectator. The way this knowledge gathered in me was the strangest thing in the world— the strangest, that is, except the very much stranger in which it quickly merged itself. . . .

She describes how she had sat down with a piece of sewing on a stone bench beside the pond and "in this position I began to take in with certitude, and yet without direct vision, the presence, at a distance, of a third person. . . ."

> There was no ambiguity in anything; none whatever, at least, in the conviction I from one moment to another found myself forming as to what I should see straight before me and across the lake as a consequence of raising my eyes.

She does not, however, raise her eyes. She continues her sewing in order to steady herself while she is deciding what to do.

63

She says that while she was sewing she knew "there was an alien object in view . . ." across the pond and this, she is convinced, is true, even though she tells herself it might be "a messenger, a postman, or a tradesman's boy," one of the men about the place. "That reminder had as little effect on my practical certitude as I was conscious—still even without looking—of its having upon the character and attitude of our visitor. Nothing was more natural than that these things should be the other things they absolutely were not." The young lady, we see, always has an abundance of "certitude." Although she has not yet looked, she would get the "positive identity of the apparition"—she tells herself—"as soon as the small clock of my courage should have ticked out the right second." She has already decided, we see, that it is an apparition. Meanwhile, she glances at little Flora. The girl is ten yards away—we are given the distance—and she expects her to cry out or to show some "sudden innocent sign either of interest or of alarm." It is difficult to understand why, since the child has her back to the water and hence her back to the "visitor" on the other bank. The girl has other things to think of; in her play she is trying to put together two pieces of wood to form a boat.

> My apprehension of what she was doing sustained me so that after some seconds I felt I was ready for more. Then I again shifted my eyes—I faced what I had to face.

This is all the evidence we have. And we are at the end of the chapter.

The first paragraph of the next chapter tells us:

I got hold of Mrs. Grose as soon after this as I could; and I can give no intelligible account of how I fought out the interval. Yet I still hear myself cry as I fairly threw myself into her arms: "They *know*—it's too monstrous: they know, they know!"

Mrs. Grose, naturally, wants to know what they know. "'Why, all that *we* know—and heaven knows what else besides!'" And she adds, "'Two hours ago, in the garden . . . Flora *saw!*'"

A supposition has now become a fact, for this is clearly not what the governess previously described. Her own fancy has quite carried her away. After telling us that Flora had her back to the Sea of Azof and was preoccupied with two pieces of wood she nevertheless tells Mrs. Grose that the girl *saw* what was on the other shore.

Mrs. Grose, true to her name, is down to earth about such matters. "'She has told you?'" she asks.

"'Not a word—that's the horror. She kept it to herself! The child of eight, *that* child!'"

Mrs. Grose persists. Her logic is sound enough: "'Then how do you know?'"

"'I was there—I saw with my eyes: saw that she was perfectly aware.'" This is a significant shift of ground—from *seeing* to her knowledge of *awareness*. She then tells Mrs. Grose that she saw across the pond a woman who was Miss Jessel.

"'How can you be sure?'" Mrs. Grose asks.

The governess says: "'Then ask Flora—*she's* sure!'"

But she has an afterthought. "'I had no sooner spoken than I caught myself up. 'No, for God's sake, *don't!* She'll

65

say she isn't—she'll lie!' "

Mrs. Grose rebels at this. " 'Ah, how *can* you?' "

" 'Because I'm clear. Flora doesn't want me to know.' "

" 'It's only then to spare you.'

" 'No, no—there are depths, depths! The more I go over it, the more I see in it, and the more I see in it the more I fear. I don't know what I *don't* see—what I *don't* fear!' "

The governess's imagination, we see, discovers "depths" within herself. Fantasy seems to be reality for her. Anything and everything can and does happen, in her mind. The attentive reader, when he is reading the story critically, can only observe that we are always in the realm of the supposititious. Not once in the entire story, do the children see anything strange or frightening. It is the governess's theory that they see as much as she does, and that they communicate with the dead. But it is the governess who does all the seeing and all the supposing. "My values are positively all blanks save only so far as an excited horror, a promoted pity, a created expertness," James explained in his Preface. But we have one significant clue to the author's "blanks." In his revision of the story for the New York Edition he altered his text again and again to put the story into the realm of the governess's feelings. Where he had her say originally "I saw" or "I believed" he often substituted "I felt."

We have here thus in reality two stories, and a method that foreshadows the problems of the stream-of-consciousness writer. One is the area of fact, the other the area of fancy. There is the witness, in this case the governess and her seemingly circumstantial story, and there is the mind itself, the contents of which are given to the reader. The reader must establish for himself the credibility of the witness; he must decide between what the governess *supposed* and what she claims she saw. Read in this fashion, *The Turn of the Screw* becomes an absorbing study of a troubled young woman, with little knowledge or understanding of children, called upon to assume serious responsibilities for the first time in her life. She finds support for her own lack of assurance by telling herself she is courageous and "wonderful." Yet in reality and by her own admission, she is filled with endless fears: "I don't know what I *don't* see—what I *don't* fear!" The life she describes at Bly is serene enough outwardly: the servants are obedient and devoted to their master and the children. The children are on the whole well behaved at Bly—and sufficiently normal to indulge in a measure of mischief. It is the governess who sees ghosts and reads sinister meanings into everything around her. It is she who subjects the children to a psychological harassment that in the end leads to Flora's hysteria and Miles's death.

In the controversies that have raged about this work, certain critics have argued that James was telling us a ghost story pure and simple, that there *are* ghosts in the tale, and that to attempt to explain the governess is to be "over-rationalistic." The ghosts, of course, are there: they belong to the experience of the governess. But to attempt to dismiss any weightier critical consideration of the tale on grounds of too much "rationalism" is to overlook the art of the narrator. Regardless of what any clinical diagnosis of the governess might be, or any judgment of her credibility as a witness, there remains her sense of horror and the extent to which it is communicated to the reader. And it is because there is this question of her feeling, and its communication to the reader, that there has been so much critical argument: for each reader feels the story differently and fills in the Jamesian blanks in accordance with these feelings. In describing Balzac's Valérie Marneffe, James spoke of the French novelist's giving her "the long rope, for her acting herself out." The governess acts herself out, that is the essence of the art used in this story. As in the case of Isabel Archer we are made aware of her "relation to herself." And by this, *The Turn of the Screw* foreshadows the psychological fiction of our century.

4

The Sacred Fount has never found the wide public of *The Turn of the Screw* and doubtless never will. For in it the narrator, in whose mind we find ourselves from beginning to end, neither engages our sympathy nor indulges in an inquiry as absorbing as the inquiry of the governess at Bly. Here, there is no prelude, no attempt to give us a setting for the story or a certain amount of data about the narrator. The reader is helpless from the start: he is confined exclusively to the evidence furnished by the one mind.

The story itself, as told to us by this unnamed man (it becomes clear early that he is a man), is an account of a fantastic attempt to worm out a series of relationships among the guests at a week-end party at a place called Newmarch. The narrator is led to believe that in the case of one couple there is physical depletion of the younger husband by his older wife. The husband has aged rapidly. It seems to the narrator, therefore, that she is becoming younger at her spouse's expense. And with his fondness for parallel situations, James creates also a man, hitherto foolish, who has now grown wise. The narrator's logical mind promptly translates this observation into a neat problem: whose "sacred fount" is this individual draining in the process of acquiring *his* superior mental capacities? The answer, obviously, is to look for a woman depleted of her wit.

And so this haunted and morbid tale plays itself out as a kind of mental detective story which is also a species of mental keyhole-peeping on the part of the narrator. He seeks to understand the relationships of the people around him about which he has such curious hypotheses and the reader is helpless—if he persists to the end—for he is caught in the trap of the narrator's calculations and conclusions. But what of the credibility of the witness? One of the characters in the story, toward the end, says to him: "'You're abused by a fine fancy.'" Again: "'You build up houses of cards.'" Again: "'. . . You over-estimate the penetration of others.'" Finally, point-blank: "'I think you're crazy.'" Some readers are inclined to agree.

This short novel of Henry James's seems to be almost a *reductio ad absurdam* of the point-of-view method. Certainly it suggests the limits beyond which a novelist may not go in presenting to the reader a character's "relation" to himself. At a given moment the narrator wonders whether it is right "'to nose about for a relation that a lady has her reasons for keeping secret.' " The fellow visitor, an artist, to whom he makes the remark, reassures him that this can be harmless, and even " 'positively honourable' " so long as the investigator adheres to " 'psychological evidence.' " He observes that " 'resting on psychologic signs alone, it's a high application of the intelligence. What's ignoble,' " he adds " 'is the detective and the keyhole.' "

The narrator accepts this gratifying rationalization and pursues his researches as a "high application of the intelligence." But he has his moments of serious doubt. Is he not the victim of a "ridiculous obsession"? He has meditated on the danger of seeking "a law that would fit certain given facts." And he warns himself against grouping these facts "into a larger mystery . . . than the facts as observed, yet warranted." As he watches the guests at dinner he feels himself "seriously warned . . . not to yield further to my idle habit of reading into mere human things an interest so much deeper than mere human things were in general prepared to supply." Yet he is vain of his faculties of observation and insight. "*I* alone was magnificently and absurdly aware—everyone else was benightedly out of it." One of the guests warns him: " 'Give up . . . the attempt to be a providence. . . . A real providence *knows;* whereas you . . . have to find out. . . .' " Her warning falls on deaf ears. The narrator congratulates himself on his "supernatural acuteness," his "plunges of insight," his "intellectual mastery" and the joy "of determining, almost of creating results!"

Almost creating results! Then he does think himself a providence! He describes himself, toward the end of the

week-end, as having created a veritable "palace of thought."
What he discovers, however, is that it is a collapsing house
of cards. For, point by point, one of the guests opposes
obvious answers to his intricate solutions. The lady tells
him " 'people have such a notion of what you embroider
on things that they're rather afraid to commit themselves
or to lead you on. . . .' " In other words even the testimony
he accumulated in talks with others is suspect. " 'You're
costing me a perfect palace of thought,' " he mourns. There
is nothing he can do. She seems to oppose to his ornate
speculations only blunt realities. "I *should* certainly never
again, on the spot, quite hang together, even though it
wasn't really that I hadn't three times her method. What I
too fatally lacked was her tone." With these words Henry
James rings down the indecisive curtain on his narrator.
Nothing has been solved, nothing settled. The reader can
only take the narrator at his ambiguous word. The narrator
has combined his curiosity with the *savoir faire* of a man
of the world who also has the sensitivity of the artist. We
have discovered he is addicted to gossip and to the intel-
lectualizing of every human situation; he seems to be prey
to anxieties unless he can achieve a kind of intellectual
superiority and omniscience over those around him. It is
this which makes him feel secure. He is kind, sympathetic,
romantic, solitary, proud—and persistent in his curiosity.
All this we can deduce. While it may be a great deal, in
terms of the narrator's personality, it tells us nothing about
the everyday facts of his life. What is his name? What does
he look like? What does he do when he isn't "nosing about"
to determine a lady's secret? As was the case with the gov-

erness of *The Turn of the Screw* we know nothing more than the person involved has told us in the process of "acting himself out." This is what Henry James meant when he wrote to H. G. Wells he had to keep the governess "impersonal." More impersonal even than the governess, is the narrator of *The Sacred Fount*.

What world are we in when we have wandered into that strange week-end at Newmarch and found ourselves totally at the mercy of the narrator, limited exclusively to his vision as we were to the governess's vision of Bly? These two works are not isolated on the long shelf of Henry James's fiction. From 1896 to the century's turn he wrote a series of studies of persons seeking to fathom the world around them and so arranged the telling of the stories that the reader must actively fathom it with them. If this is the method of the drama, it is also the method of the traditional detective story. The works follow in a logical progression: *What Maisie Knew*, in which the reader must determine how much a "light vessel of consciousness," a little girl, knew of the world of divorce and adultery into which she was thrown; *The Turn of the Screw*, with the governess seeking to fathom the world at Bly largely created by herself; the little telegraph girl of "In the Cage," piecing together from her limited angle of vision the meanings of the messages she dispatches in her capacity as clerk in a telegraph office; *The Awkward Age*, in which the heroine, emerging from late adolescence, tries to put together the meaning of the adult world into which her mother prematurely thrusts her; and finally *The Sacred Fount*. James admitted that these characters all possess a "rage of wonderment." The reader must acquire the same "rage," for in each case, with the exception of *The Awkward Age,* we remain largely within the given "point of view." The reader's mind is forced to hold to two levels of awareness: *the story as told,* and *the story to be deduced.* This is the calculated risk Henry James took in writing for audiences not prepared to read him so actively. The writer of stream of consciousness takes the same risk.

5

In locating his angle of vision in one specific consciousness, or in a series of reflecting minds, James anticipated most of the problems of the stream-of-consciousness writers. One more step was needed: this was the creation of the illusion that the reader actually follows the character's flowing thought. There are moments in James—"The Jolly Corner" comes to mind—when he has virtually written a kind of internal monologue. In his work, however, he selects not only the thoughts, analyzing them at times in a manner that foreshadows Proust, but he is deeply concerned over the kind of consciousness he will present to the reader. There was no merit, James argued, in mirroring the consciousness of the "headlong fools" of this world. In a long work it was necessary to find an illuminating intelligence, capable of contributing the greatest interest and the deepest understanding of the life the author wished to recreate. Such an intelligence becomes a sensitive register, a receptacle of the lucidity to be imparted to the reader. The novelist, however, did not rule out the interest for fiction of a more limited intelligence in a given case, and he warned against "filling too full any supposed and above all limited vessel of consciousness."

Concretely James saw that the psychological novelist is primarily concerned with "what a man thinks and what he feels." These constituted, he wrote, "the history and the character of what he does." "The figures in any picture," said James, "the agents in any drama, are interesting only in proportion as they feel their respective situations." With that need for fine distinction, he discussed the different degrees of feeling: the muffled and the faint, the just-sufficient, the "barely intelligent" as against "the acute, the intense, the complete." For the *leading* interest" in a novel James preferred a "finely aware" character—aware as Hamlet was, or Lear. His invocation of Hamlet and Lear might give us pause. Was not James adapting a very old concept to his contemporary world? The old drama-tists chose the struggles and conflicts of kings and queens for their subjects since the essence of classical tragedy was the fall of a person of high estate. James sought to create superior minds to give his dramas nobler themes, finer sub-stance, higher tension. For him there had to be—in a large work— a "consciousness subject to fine intensification and wide enlargement. It is as mirrored in that consciousness that the gross fools, the headlong fools, the fatal fools play their part for us—they have much less to show us in them-selves."

Some critics have fallen into the habit of saying that James ruled out the "fools" of this world from his fiction save as reflected elements of life. This of course is to mis-read what he said; moreover there are fools in abundance in his work. It is important for us to understand that James was expressing a preference for an illuminating intelligence as a *"leading* interest"—the italic was his—"at the centre of our subject." Elsewhere in the same passage he very clearly says "I think no 'story' is possible without its fools."

The generalization for the contemporary psychological novelist in this careful Jamesian theorizing may be stated as follows: from the moment we are inside the mind of a character we are committed to that character's *point of view.* It follows that the more intense the perceiver, the more intense the experience of the reader. The writer must be aware of the limits of the consciousness he is projecting: he must not make a limited mind too perceptive, nor impose limitations where there is abundant capacity for perception. Each consciousness, in other words, must be kept consistent within itself. Faulkner's Benjy is an admirable illustration of the careful observance of James's admonitions.

IV

THE INTERNAL MONOLOGUE

WE HAVE SEEN HOW DIFFICULT IT IS FOR THE NOVELIST TO set down in words a record of inner experience. It has been no less difficult for criticism to find adequate terms to describe this literary process. William James chose the metaphor "stream of consciousness" only after discarding "chain of thought" and "train of thought"—both phrases seeming to him to suggest too much the idea that thought is jointed. "A 'river' or a 'stream' are the metaphors by which it is most naturally described," he wrote. "In talking of it hereafter, let us call it the stream of thought, of consciousness or of subjective life." Since the writing of these words, criticism has fumbled without success for an adequate, all-inclusive label. A series of "interior" labels was devised: interior vision, interior cinema, interior or internal monologue—and it is the latter which has acquired considerable currency. (James Joyce, with his characteristic genius for adding a wry verbal twist to such phrases turns it, in *Finnegans Wake*, into "the steady monologuy of the interiors.")

When Joyce singled out Édouard Dujardin as the originator of the internal monologue, the French novelist—after the fact—delivered the lecture in which he attempted to define what he had discovered half a century before. This was published with the portentous title: *Le monologue intérieur, son apparition, ses origines, sa place dans l'oeuvre de James Joyce et dans le roman contemporain.* It is something less than the treatise the title suggests; and Dujardin actually speaks of it as an "attempt" at a definition. His general conclusions are:

> The internal monologue, like every monologue, is the speech of a given character, designed to introduce us directly into the internal life of this character, without the author's intervening by explaining or commenting, and like every monologue, is a discourse without listener and a discourse unspoken;
>
> but it differs from the traditional monologue in that:
>
> as regards its substance, it expresses the most intimate thoughts, those closest to the unconscious;
>
> as regards its spirit, it is discourse prior to all logical organization, reproducing thought in its original state and as it comes into the mind,
>
> as for its form, it is expressed by means of direct sentences reduced to a syntactic minimum;
>
> thus it responds essentially to the conception which we have today of poetry.

From this analysis, serving as preamble, he derives the following more concise definition:

> The internal monologue, in its nature on the order of poetry, is that unheard and unspoken speech by which a character expresses his inmost thoughts, those lying nearest the unconscious, without regard to logical organization—that is, in their original state—by means of direct sentences reduced to syntactic minimum, and in such a way as to give

the impression of reproducing the thoughts just as they come into the mind.

The preamble and definition mix things up somewhat. It is confusing to have the word "speech" or "discourse" introduced in alluding to something "unheard and unspoken." Use of the words implies also that we think always on the verbal level whereas the "thoughts just as they come into the mind," as Dujardin himself recognized, sensory, image-laden and fragmented, are often beyond words. Above all, the concept that "internal monologue" expresses those thoughts "closest to the unconscious" suggests a misunderstanding of the nature of the unconscious. Stephen Spender makes exactly the same mistake in *The Destructive Element* when he labels the chapter devoted to Joyce and James "The Unconscious."

The present inquiry is concerned exclusively with consciousness as rendered in fiction: but it is necessary to make clear the distinction between consciousness and the unconscious which can never be rendered but only deduced.

There are few things more difficult to explain than the unconscious. Many persons, indeed, deny its existence even though there has been an awareness of it, in greater or lesser degree, from early times. It was not invented by Freud, as some would have us believe. The teachings of modern psychology have shown (and we have daily evidence of it in our own lives if we know how to observe it), that an unconscious level of experience is constituted within us whose *conscious* patterns may be read only by those especially qualified to do so. We ourselves are vouch-safed only occasional glimpses into it. It can be read only in terms of those thoughts and fantasies which we bring *into consciousness*. I think I can offer an illustration. There exists an unpublished letter at Harvard University written by Henry James in 1884. In it he promises a serial to the editor of the *Atlantic Monthly* for the year 1885. However, three times in this letter, so clearly of 1884, Henry James makes the same slip of the pen: he writes 1865 instead of 1885 as the year for which he promises the serial. Had it happened once, we might lay it to inadvertence; but thrice, and then uncorrected, means that James's *unconscious* substituted 1865 for 1885, and he remained unaware of what he had done. I exclude the possibility of conscious intention since there was no palpable reason for giving a wrong year in a serious business letter. *The slip of the pen, therefore, was a clear signature of his unconscious.* We can formulate as many theories as we like about the reasons for this slip of the pen; but all we can say definitely is that some part of James's unconscious led his hand to write a wrong year not once but thrice—a year two decades removed from the year he wanted to write. The record itself is no longer unconscious, since we can see it and recognize it; the "1865" is the symbol by which we recognize some element in the Jamesian unconscious.

In a word, the unconscious cannot be expressed in its own unconscious form, since obviously this is unconscious. *We can only infer it from symbols emerging in the conscious expressions of the person,* such as remembered dreams, fantasies, or slips of the tongue or of the pen. Thus when Édouard Dujardin speaks of the area "closest the unconscious," what he is really referring to is that peripheral area, outside the central stream of thought, to which we do not always attend, but which is the "halo" or " fringe" of impression described by William James. The use of the word "unconscious" by Dujardin can only create confusion. It takes us to areas which are beyond rendering save in some substitutive, symbolic *but still conscious* form.

2

The term "internal monologue" was used at first interchangeably with the term "stream of consciousness." Harry Levin, in his critical study of Joyce, expressed a preference for it, stating that "the internal monologue lends itself more readily to critical analysis than the more illusory stream of consciousness." Neither term covers all cases; one or the other can be used as a critical convenience; but it must be recognized that the word "monologue," because of its association with the theatre, has distinct literary and dramatic connotations that do not convey the idea of flux. In the traditional monologue—in its original Greek sense it was a "speaking alone"—the character gives the audience logical and reasoned thoughts. These are "structured" even while they represent inner reflection or reverie, and are rendered without relation to external stimuli. Hamlet's "To be or not to be . . ." read by itself, out of the context of the play, gives us no feeling of his surroundings or the sensory experiences he may be having at the time of utterance. His monologue, or soliloquy, reflects and expresses his inner tension, the conflicts of his troubled spirit: his

measured thoughts have been distilled from the fluid stream
of consciousness to which, in this case, we have no access,
since all the impurities have been filtered out. If, by
making a pastiche of Shakespeare and Joyce, we were to
insert some of the impurities, the result would certainly
be neither what Shakespeare nor Joyce would have intended, but it serves to illustrate our point:

> To be or not to be that is the question
> The ghost—th' agenbite of inwit; he pandied me!
> What is this stench? the slings, the arrows, ah! cruel
> Outrageous fortune. Clang! Who tolls the bell?
> Modality ineluctable. To sleep
> Perchance to dream; aye there's the rub . . .

Here Hamlet is no longer organizing thought: ideas come
to him by association: the memory of his father's ghost reminds him of the bite of inner guilt; some recollection of
a boyish punishment, perhaps related to the feeling of
guilt. Then an unpleasant odor is noticed, but his mind
jumps from this to the slings and arrows—the cruel ups
and downs—of one's fortunes and a clanging bell impinges
upon this thought. From the bell his mind leaps to the
ineluctable modality of the visible and the blessing of
sleep which erases the visible and substitutes dreams. In
a word, our pastiche is monologue to which has been added
the direct verbal expression of associations and sensory
perceptions. The words "internal monologue" inadequately
describe the fluid and unstructured state of thought we
have tried to suggest as existing in Hamlet's mind. The
descriptive words "stream of consciousness" seem more
apposite.

Eugene O'Neill, in *Strange Interlude*, probably under the influence of the writings of Joyce, made a direct attempt to introduce stream of consciousness on the stage. As produced by the Theatre Guild, the play consisted of the usual speeches of the characters, who also, however, spoke their thoughts using a different vocal inflection. All action on stage was momentarily arrested and frozen, while the thoughts were uttered. In doing this, however, O'Neill was employing merely the time-honored "asides" of the old plays or a series of soliloquies. Thus at the beginning of the play Marsden enters. His spoken speech is "I'll wait in here, Mary," and then we are ushered into his thoughts:

> How perfectly the Professor's unique haven! . . . Primly classical . . . when New Englander meets Greek! . . . He hasn't added one book in years . . . how old was I when I first came here? . . . six . . . with my father . . . father . . . how dim his face has grown! . . . he wanted to speak to me just before he died . . . the hospital . . . smell of iodoform in the cool halls . . . hot summer . . . I bent down . . . his voice had withdrawn far away . . . I couldn't understand him . . . what son can ever understand? . . . always too near, too soon, too distant or too late. . . .

The thought associations in this passage are rendered in a fairly logical progression; what we are given essentially is a chain of memory without intrusion of external stimuli and no representation of peripheral thought. This can be called "internal monologue." Nevertheless we must recognize that whatever critical terms we may apply to O'Neill's experiment, he seems to have created the illusion for the play's audiences that they were participating in the mental life of the characters.

We must not lose ourselves in a search for label-definitions; nor should we attempt to make them tightly fit certain works that can better be described than labeled. The term "internal monologue" becomes merely a useful designation for certain works of fiction of sustained subjectivity, written from a single point of view, in which the writer himself narrows down the stream of consciousness and places us largely at the "center" of the character's thoughts—that center where thought often uses words rather than images. To understand the problems involved alike for writer and reader we can turn to Dujardin's pioneer experiment. It has many things to teach us about the psychological novel of our time.

V

A SYMBOLIST EXPERIMENT

THE EXTENT TO WHICH ÉDOUARD DUJARDIN ERECTED HIS definition of "internal monologue" *post factum* becomes clear when we read *Les lauriers sont coupés,* which in translation by Stuart Gilbert was called *We'll to the Woods No More.* One gains the impression from it that Dujardin arrived at his definition as much from a reading of Joyce as from a rereading of himself. In dismissing his novel as slight and unimportant criticism has overlooked the singular historical interest of the work and the illumination it casts upon a writer's struggle to render flowing thought. James Joyce, in advising Valéry Larbaud to read the book, told him that he would find himself "from the very first line, posted within the mind of the protagonist." Larbaud quoted Joyce as saying: "It is the continuous unfolding of his thoughts which, replacing normal objective narration, depicts to us his acts and experiences."

The entire book is quotation from the mind of its hero. Dujardin recognized that to create an illusion of mental flux he would have to give an effect of thoughts entering his hero's mind at random. On the other hand, he struggled constantly with the problem of setting his scenes and carrying on the action. Let us walk with Dujardin's hero into a restaurant (as we will later do with Joyce's Leopold Bloom). We do not yet know his name. That will be revealed to us progressively in the later pages of the book. We know that on this soft, warm April evening in Paris he has a rendezvous with an actress. We know that the year is 1887, since in the opening pages, the hero was told by a friend that he intended to see *Ruy Blas* that very evening at the Théâtre-Français and the thought that entered the hero's mind was: "The idea of going to see *Ruy Blas* in 1887!" We know it is a warm, soft April evening because, rather opportunely, that was in the hero's thought in the opening paragraphs of the book.

> Red and gold [he has entered the restaurant], a glare of light, the café; flashing mirrors; a white-aproned waiter; pillars hung with hats and overcoats. Anyone here I know? Those people are watching me come in; a thin chap with long whiskers, looks the regular heavy father. All the tables taken, where shall I sit? An empty place down there, capital, my usual table; why shouldn't a fellow have his favourite table? Nothing for Leah to laugh at in that.
> —Yes, sir?
> The waiter. The table. My hat on the peg. Take gloves off; drop them casually on the table, beside the plate; or shall I in my overcoat pocket? No, on the table; it's trifles like that show a fellow's style. Hang up my coat now; sit down; that's better; really fagged I was. Yes, I'll put my gloves in the overcoat pocket after all. . . .

The scene has its parallel—much more intricately written—in *Ulysses*. The internal monologue here can only be described as "primitive" and yet it conveys a sufficient degree of reality. It is not altogether convincing to have us believe that the preoccupied man would necessarily bring into the center of his consciousness the table, the hat on the peg, the removal of his gloves; these would be registered almost automatically by anyone who has removed his gloves many times before or placed his hat on many pegs in many restaurants. This said, it must be acknowledged that such thoughts are conceivable in a person self-consciously concerned about the figure he is cutting in the presence of the other diners. In terms of fictional verisimilitude the thoughts—waiter, table, hat on peg, gloves—seem to be serving as the equivalent of stage directions in a play, and the hero figures as an actor, whose every move has been calculated. But the reality would be a simultaneous registering of the items tabulated by Dujardin in the hero's mind, and doubtless beyond the verbal level.

Dujardin incorporates into the monologue not only these "stage directions," but his scenic descriptions. At the opening of the book:

> The hour is striking six, the hour I waited for. Here is the house I have to enter, where I shall meet someone; the house; the hall; let's go in.

Once he is inside:

> . . . The stairs; the first steps. Supposing he has left early; he sometimes does; but I have got to tell him the story of my day. The first landing; wide, bright staircase; windows. . . .

The only non-descriptive thought, indeed the only genuine reflection in this passage that has some logic on the verbal level is "Supposing he has left early. . . ."

91

We can readily observe Dujardin maneuvering to remain inside his hero's mind while seeking to impart to the reader the data customarily given by the omniscient author in conventional fiction. Midway through the book the effort breaks down. The reader is not yet in possession of the complete story of the hero's romance with the actress. Feeling still the need to impart every last detail, Dujardin grafts onto his text a reading by Daniel Prince (it is in this portion that we discover his name) of all the letters he has received from the object of his affection. From this correspondence we learn the extent of his vanity and the way in which he is the dupe of the actress. We learn also of the fascination she exercises upon him.

The narrative awkwardnesses must not be allowed to distract us from the positive elements in the work. If we begin with a sense of impatience and a feeling that Dujardin has willy-nilly made a grab-bag of image and phrase in Prince's mind, we find ourselves by degrees gathered into the story, pulled along in it by a certain charm as well as by the suspense aroused by Dujardin—the suspense of whether on this night Daniel Prince will succeed in his amatory quest. We have a very real, and even acute, sense of being in the Paris of 1887; we feel the softness of the evening on the boulevards, we saunter with the hero in his top hat and his gloves, we are aware of his self-consciousness, we gape with him at the girls, we light the candle in his dressing room and almost feel the fresh cold water he splashes on his face. And finally, standing with him on his balcony, we are caught up in the atmosphere of his mind and in his reverie:

I lean on the balcony, bending over the emptiness of space; I take deep breaths of the evening air, vaguely conscious of that loveliness outside, the shadowed, soft, forlorn remoteness of the air, all this night's beauty; a grey-black sky, here and there suffused with blue, and tiny stars, like tremulous drops of water, watery stars; all around, the misty paleness of open sky; over yonder a solid gloom of trees and, beyond, black houses with lighted windows; roofs, dingy roofs; below, blurred together, the garden; a chaos of tangled walls and all sorts of things; black houses with lighted windows; and, above me, the sky, vast, bluish, whitened with its early stars; mild air, no wind, air warm with the breath of early May. There is warmth, a soft caress, in this velvety night air; the trees down there are a patch of gloom beneath the grey-blue circle of sky, spangled with tremulous gleams; and vague shadows brood in the garden of night.

This may seem more like description of a series of images than of thought. The passage, however, is evocative, and it assumes reality for us because we are by now firmly inside the mind of Daniel Prince. We are looking with Prince from his balcony: what he mirrors for us, we see. Gradually the form of the actress (in Daniel's mind—and ours) merges with the night:

I see your beauty and your grace; divinely graceful as you move, the even cadence of your limbs; and languid your steps on the carpet beside the table with the flowers, in your delicious yellow room, yes, languidly you walk across a sheen of flowered softness, slowly leaning now this way, now that, palely smiling, your ivory face framed in frolic gold, smiling, slowly swaying as you pass, you pass before me; your light gown of creamy muslin floats about you, rippling where a ribbon flutters, gathered muslin moulding your bosom, your limbs, the young grace of your body; and softly your lips are moving; lovedear, I love you so. Tall shadows of trees climb skywards, high on high; and mine, all mine, you glimmer in the pale shadows, smiling, simple sweet and kind. . . .

What is clear from these passages is that Dujardin, the symbolist and friend of Mallarmé, although writing a novel that is a projection of symbolist theory—the rendering of the evanescence of experience—actually tries to set down in concrete terms the sense perceptions of his hero which generally are not expressed on a verbal level. With few exceptions the words he uses are not highly imaged or nuanced, but direct and concrete. If the book is not rich in the metaphors we have come to regard as an integral part of symbolist expression, it does seem to be indulging in what might best be described as a kind of *impressionism.* As Daniel leans over the balcony, the scene he looks at, reflected in his mind, can remind one of an impressionist painting. Perhaps the only symbolist touch one finds in the passage itself is Daniel's image of the stars as "tremulous drops of water."

One passage comes closer to what we might call stream-of-consciousness writing than the recording of internal monologue. In the warmth of the actress's room, and with her head on his shoulder, the young hero floats away into a daydream that carries him to the verge of sleep. It makes us wonder whether he does not prefer his dream of the actress to the reality of making love to her:

. . . this is her body; the rise and fall of her breast, her blended fragrance, oh lovely April night! . . . Presently we

94

shall be driving together . . . in cool air . . . we will go out . . . quite soon . . . the two candles . . . along the boulevards . . . *I love my turkeys and my sheep, But oh I love you more.* . . . That street girl with the bold eyes and cherry lips . . . the room, high fireplace . . . the dining room . . . my father . . . sitting together, we three, father, mother, I . . . why is mother so pale? . . . she is watching me . . . we shall dine, yes, in the garden . . . the servant . . . bring the table . . . Leah . . . she is laying the table . . . my father . . . the concierge . . . with a letter . . . a letter from her? . . . thanks . . . a ripple, a murmur, skies uprising, high on high. . . .

In this novel we discover again that we must read on two levels of awareness: we can, if we achieve identification with Daniel Prince, ride with him in the carriage beside the beautiful woman; but we are also appraising him—standing off from him, evaluating his own testimony, and seeing him from the outside for the dupe that he is. He emerges as a character both *felt* and seen: we watch his self-intoxication and note his vanity and his illusions; we also sense the Paris around him, all early spring and soft, and are aware of a time removed from our own. As we turn back over the pages of the book we discover we have lived the story in spite of its absurdities: the novel has conveyed an atmosphere, created a character, given us an almost uncanny time-sense, teased our mind with a gentle curiosity: will Daniel Prince succeed in his amatory quest on this night in 1887 or will the actress rebuff him anew?

Any account of such a novel represents a pulling-together of disparate elements of the story. It is in *my* mind that the disorderly thoughts, presented out of sequence, have been reshuffled into some semblance of order. In reading this novel, in listening to Daniel Prince's internal monologue with a third ear, I have rewritten the novel. The question that now must be asked is this: Would all readers read such novels in a similar manner?

VI

THE
READER'S VISION

WOULD ALL READERS READ SUCH NOVELS IN A SIMILAR manner? The question is at the very heart of our inquiry.

There are, in Proust, certain admirable pages on the reading of fiction. In real life, he observes, people are too opaque, they represent too much physical mass, too much of a "dead weight which our sensibilities have not the strength to lift." People in books, however, are more readily assimilated. Since our experience of people, in life or in books, is through our mind and our feelings, the fictitious persons can take on a reality more intense than the real persons for "we have made them our own, since it is in ourselves that they are happening." And Proust goes on to say:

> . . . Once the novelist has brought us to that state, in which, as in all purely mental states, every emotion is multiplied ten-fold, into which his book comes to disturb us as might a dream, but a dream more lucid, and of a more lasting impression, than those which come to us in sleep; why, then, for the space of an hour he sets free within us all the joys and sorrows in the world, a few of which, only, we should have to spend years of our actual life in getting to know, and the keenest, the most intense of which would

99

never have been revealed to us because the slow course of their development stops our perception of them.

Thus Proust discovered, as Henry James had done before him, that the writer of fiction can not only represent life but actually can create it for a reader—a reader sufficiently attentive and responsive to what he is reading.

An important distinction must be drawn between the material most readers can grasp in a novel and that part of it which becomes, in effect, a part of our personal mental dream-state. We all read the same words on the printed page and gather from them a similar meaning; our intellect grasps the essential content and the data furnished by the novelist; we can discuss the book with another reader in perfect agreement as to the kind of story it has to tell. But the question recurs: do we *experience* the book in the same way? How many persons have felt terror upon reading a ghostly tale such as *The Turn of the Screw* only to discover, in surprise, that a fellow reader "couldn't get through the book"? How many readers have shed real tears over some trivial romantic book they knew to be unreal, while other readers shrugged their shoulders and laughed? Between the book *read* and the book *felt* there lie all the differences of opinion that divide reader and reader, critic and critic. Rare are the readers who can achieve a balance between intellectual apprehension of a novel and an intense feeling of it. Yet it is for the feeling as much as the intellectual apprehension that most novelists write their work.

This is particularly true of the modern psychological novel. Here the entire work, by its very nature, offers us the data in higgledy-piggledy disorder. We are asked to *see into* the characters, to make deductions from such data as may be offered us—and at the same time to *live* for ourselves the experience with which we are confronted on the printed page. This is asking a great deal of the reader and it explains why encounters between writers and readers (on the printed page) are so varied and so contradictory. The critical reader who intellectually apprehends a book but has achieved no particular feeling in the process usually has only a ledger-book concept of the work. He can retell the story, give the ages of the characters or describe what they look like, discourse upon the logic of the tale told, yet his discourse will be comparatively lifeless—though it may be as exact as figures in a ledger or statistics in a document. At the other extreme is the reader who has *felt* every page of the work, but can give us no coherent account of the data and is happy even to be able to give a reasonable account (difficult enough at any time) of the experience of the reading.

2

Let us look at Dorothy Richardson's *Pointed Roofs*, the first volume or "chapter" of her twelve-volume *Pilgrimage*.* About the entire work there are extremes of opinion— some readers find it unreadable and "impossible" while others speak of it with high emotion. Whether we are able to read it or not we must accept its "pioneer" place in the history of the twentieth century novel. Miss Richardson set herself a difficult experiment, perhaps more difficult in a

* The volumes are titled: *Pointed Roofs, Backwater, Honeycomb, The Tunnel, Interim, Deadlock, Revolving Lights, The Trap, Oberland, Dawn's Left Hand, Clear Horizon, Dimple Hill.*

technical sense than Proust's: like her French contemporary she placed the reader in the mind of a single character, and with great tenacity of purpose held to her difficult task until it was completed. The twelve "chapters" deal exclusively with the pilgrimage of Miriam Henderson's mind from adolescence to middle life.

At this point in the inquiry it seems to me that I can best discuss the entire question of the reader's relation to the novel of subjectivity by drawing upon my own experience in the reading of *Pointed Roofs*. I read it first two decades ago and found I could develop no interest in Miriam Henderson and her emotional adventures in the German boarding school to which she goes to teach the English language. The volume indeed discouraged me from reading any of its successors and it seemed to me that the great defect of the book was that Dorothy Richardson had selected too dull a mind for her experiment.

Returning to *Pointed Roofs* after two decades, I found once more that my interest lagged. The author was involving me in a world of chirping females and I had to force myself to absorb the contents of each page. The heroine struck me as immature and wholly without interest. I had begun by imagining her in the first pages as a rather prim Victorian type, perhaps twenty-five, who had just packed her new Saratoga trunk and was being escorted with Victorian decorum to her first job, on the Continent, in a German school at Hanover. The sense of her being an older person despite her youthful behavior seemed confirmed when after about fifty pages "Miriam sat up stiffly— adjusted her pince-nez—and desperately ordered the reading to begin again." It was, however, difficult to relate this Miriam of the pince-nez to the Miriam constantly being revealed in the book, a creature of variable moods, now measured and grave, now mercurial.

I had read almost a hundred pages when I suddenly encountered this startling (to me) sentence: "She could do nothing even with these girls, and she was nearly eighteen." Miriam, wearing her Victorian pince-nez is not yet eighteen! (She turns eighteen and puts up her hair for the first time in the opening pages of the second volume, *Backwater*.) Thus my whole judgment of the first volume had been colored by an erroneous impression produced by the pince-nez, the Saratoga trunk and the "grown-up" airs assumed by Miriam.

In a conventional novel I would have known Miriam Henderson's age from the start. I would have understood clearly those moods of late adolescence, the chirping scenes of the opening pages which had reminded me of the novels of Louisa May Alcott, the general ecstatic quality of some of the passages of her internal monologue. But the picture was blurred; I was reading the novel with an unfocused vision. What was more, even after it was clear to me that Miriam was not yet eighteen, the full effect of this revelation did not sink in promptly. It was a gradual process, requiring a slow focusing of my own mental pince-nez. Looking back across the pages to rediscover my experience as a reader, I found the scene, the important scene, in which the book quite suddenly changed in my hands from a lifeless dead weight of paper and print, to a living thing, from a work I was intellectually absorbing, and finding

tedious, to a work charged with feeling and life. It occurred when I began to reread certain sections of the book
in the light of my newly-acquired picture of Miriam.

The particular scene that performed the curious change
in my relationship to the book occurs when Miriam, in a
mood of elation, is singing to herself that she will be going
to visit "Pom-pom-pom-er-ania" and bursts into the school
hall there to discover the Swiss Pastor Lahmann near the
window. " 'You are vairy happy, mademoiselle,' " he says to
her. She responds in a way to which we have become ac-
customed: she likes men, but they also frighten her. She
likes the pastor's "comforting black mannishness" and at
the same time is so put off by him that she blandly denies
she is in a happy mood. The pastor quietly talks to her and
remarks among other things that he has a fondness for the
English verse,

> "A little land, well-tilled,
> A little wife, well-willed,
> And great riches."

Miriam seemed to gaze long at a pallid, rounded man
with smiling eyes. She saw a garden and fields, a firelit interior, a little woman smiling and busy and agreeable moving quickly about . . . and Pastor Lahmann—presiding.
It filled her with fury to be regarded as one of a world of
little tame things to be summoned by little men to be well-
willed wives. She must make him see that she did not even
recognize such a thing as 'a well-willed wife.' She felt her
gaze growing fixed and moved to withdraw it and herself.

But the pastor quite suddenly changes the subject.

"Why do you wear glasses, mademoiselle?"
The voice was full of sympathetic wistfulness.

"I have a severe myopic astigmatism," she announced, gathering up her music and feeling the words as little hammers on the newly seen, pallid, rounded face.

"Dear me . . . I wonder whether the glasses are really necessary. . . . May I look at them? . . . I know something of eye-work."

Miriam detached her tightly fitting pince-nez and, having given them up, stood with her music in hand anxiously watching. Half her vision gone with her glasses, she saw only a dim black-coated knowledge, near at hand, going perhaps to help her.

"You wear them always—for how long?"

"Poor child, poor child, and you must have passed through all your schooling with those lame, lame eyes . . . let me see the eyes . . . turn a little to the light . . . so."

Standing near and large he scrutinized her vague gaze.

"And sensitive to light, too. You were vairy, vairy blonde, even more blonde than you are now, as a child, mademoiselle?"

"Na guten tag, Herr Pastor."

Fräulein Pfaff's smiling voice sounded from the little door.

Pastor Lahmann stepped back.

Now the book was alive for me, not only because there had been a moment of drama, an encounter between an adolescent English girl with a benign and paternal Swiss pastor, but because in some way some quality of feeling had disengaged itself from the pages—or been disengaged within me. What had performed this extraordinary change, so that now I could see Miriam, see the schoolroom, hear the pastor's accent, feel sorry for her near-sightedness and her uneasiness with men? I turned to other passages. Everywhere now Miriam was real, palpable; formerly-dull pages warmed into new interest and new life. I went back and started the book from the beginning. Now I was able to read it through with no sense of tedium. Delicate shades of feeling were there, and moments of the heroine's experience—sunsets, a storm, the very sense of Hanover's streets, the rigidities of Fräulein Pfaff, the music in the evenings, the tremulous awarenesses of the young girls in the school—all this which had seemed inconsequential before now had validity, even though the book had no story and nothing happened that was not part of the ordinary events in a girls' school, such as the girls washing their hair, or talking about their boy friends.

What had happened? It was important to understand. And as I searched the memory of my own reading it seemed to me that I had somehow begun by struggling against Dorothy Richardson: she had wanted me to enter into the mind of a young adolescent—a female adolescent—and I had not been able to do this. I could not adopt the one "point of view" she offered me, an angle of vision that required more identification than I—as indeed many of her male readers—could achieve. It is doubtless much easier for a man to enter into the mind of Daniel Prince going to a rendezvous with an actress than the mind of a moody young English girl in a German girls' school. The episode with Pastor Lahmann, however, had offered me the key. And as I studied it closely I saw that what had happened here was that *through* Miriam Henderson's angle of vision of the pastor I had finally entered the book. She had made me aware of him and it was with him I could identify. So that while we see him only as Miriam sees him, it became possible suddenly for me, the male reader, to feel myself

standing in front of this blond English girl and inquiring
into her near-sightedness. The alchemy of this was that—
as Proust observed, "since it is in ourselves that they are
happening"—Miriam now became real for me and remained real. At last I could experience her as Dorothy
Richardson doubtless wanted me to: a near-sighted English girl translated between a certain March and July from
Victorian London to a German school, experiencing the
strangeness of the German world, swinging between
euphoria and depression, reaching out with the heightened
sensitivity of adolescence to her environment, experiencing
assaults of feeling in her relationships with the girls in the
school, uncertain of her feelings about men. The general
effect of the book—and the feelings I had contributed to
my rereading of it—seemed to have brought me close to
the reality Dorothy Richardson had sought to create.

3

This was my experience as a persistent and searching
reader. It was not at all clear that any generalization could
be made from this experience. I did, however, feel that it
might be fruitful to ask for the testimony of other readers.
I had noted the extent to which some of the male members
of my Princeton Seminar had actually resented being maneuvered by Dorothy Richardson into the mind of an
adolescent girl. On the other hand, a woman student in
my seminar at New York University spoke of Miriam's
mind as "a delicate instrument" and described the excite-
ment experienced in observing the heroine through the
"peep-holes of her mind." A distinguished English novelist,
a woman, told me that reading Dorothy Richardson had

been one of the richest experiences of her youth. An American poet, a woman, described to me how she had read the book not as a whole, but by discovering Miriam's emotions and her sensual and perceptual experiences from page to page. And on seeing Miss Richardson's volumes in the home of another woman, she also a poet, I pursued my inquiry by asking what her reading of these books had yielded her. The incisive reply was "intensities."

Perhaps the only generalization possible then is that in a novel which uses internal monologue as Dorothy Richardson did, the author succeeds only when the reader achieves a certain state of identification or relationship with the sole mind that is offered to him on the pages of the book. But I suspect also that for the many the problem lies in the need to see a wholeness that can be achieved only after all the disparate facts have been gathered. This is what Joseph Frank meant when he observed that a stream-of-consciousness novel cannot be "read" in the usual sense— it only can be reread. In rereading we have the heightened awareness that has come to us from what was at first not so much a reading of the book as an exploration of its content. This, however, must be slightly amended to include the experience of the two women poets who, in the real sense, *read* the book, without the need for rereading. For them, I suppose, there was no need to grasp the continuum of Miriam's experience—since the poet may focus his attention on a flower, a tree, a bird, a cloud, discovering beauty in each and making of each a wholeness complete in itself. Or, to return to the stream image, they can float on the stream of consciousness seeing only what is in the stream at a given moment without the need to look behind to see what has gone before or to know the direction that is being taken.

4

Dorothy Richardson offered no theories about her work. The experiment itself sufficed. In an interview she once expressed her dissatisfaction with the phrase "stream of consciousness," asserting that "amongst the company of useful labels devised to meet the exigencies of literary criticism it stands alone, isolated by its perfect imbecility." And she went on to give her concept of the flux of experience which amounted to a description of what she had tried to convey in her rendering of Miriam Henderson's mind:

> The 'mind' may be or may become, anything from a rag-bag to a mad-house. It may wobble continuously or may be more or less steadily focused. But its central core, luminous point (call it what you will, its names are legion) tho' more or less continuously expanding from birth to maturity, remains stable, one with itself throughout life.

Her novel is, indeed, built around a series of "luminous points"—what the poet described as "intensities"—and Miriam Henderson remains most of the time the "central core." A heightened awareness of Miriam should not blind us to the limitations of Dorothy Richardson's creation. We can sometimes feel ourselves to be trapped spectators in the mind of a woman possessing no marked personality, often sentimental and belligerently feminine and rather unimaginative, yet having extraordinary flashes of insight which redeem many turgid pages. Miss Richardson's literary style improved in the later volumes, but great plateaus of aridity surround the "intensities." However, she opened a new pathway, cleared the ground, exerted an unmistakable influence.

When she gathered together the twelve parts of *Pilgrimage* into a four-volume collected edition in 1938 she wrote a rather elliptical Foreword to the series. In it she described how the choice for her, in 1911, when she started writing, was between realists like Balzac and her contemporary Arnold Bennett, or men who were writing novels of satire and protest. She determined to produce "a feminine equivalent of the current masculine realism" but became aware, as she wrote, of "a stranger in the form of contemplated reality having for the first time . . . its own way." This "contemplated reality" revealed a hundred faces "any of which, the moment it was entrapped within the close mesh of direct statement, summoned its fellows to disqualify it." She acknowledged that Henry James might have taught her how to keep "the reader incessantly watching the conflict of human forces through the eye of a single observer." However, she suggests that Goethe had long ago defined the subjective novel:

> In the novel [wrote Goethe] reflections and incidents should be featured; in drama character and action. The novel must proceed slowly and the thought processes of the principal figure must, by one device or another, hold up the development of the whole . . .

What Dorothy Richardson stated in her Preface, which was probably her final word on the subject, is to be found in another form in *Dawn's Left Hand,* the tenth "chapter" of *Pilgrimage.* She speaks here of the "self-satisfied, complacent, know-all condescendingness" which she contends James and Conrad displayed in their handling of their materials. Wells seemed to her "to have more awareness," but, she observes, "all his books are witty exploitations of ideas." And she adds "The torment of *all* novels is what is left out. . . . Bang, bang, bang, on they go, these men's books, like an L.C.C. tram, yet unable to make you forget them, the authors, for a moment."

What novels left out, if we are to judge by what Dorothy Richardson put in, are whole areas of feeling, the self-absorbing reverie, combined with acute perceptual experience. The swings in mood of the heroine serve only to intensify our awareness of reality; out of this alternation of the evanescent and the concrete, Miriam ultimately emerges a rounded, one might say a three-dimensional figure—just so long as we can stay with her and bear up under certain inevitable *longueurs*—stay with her and *feel* with her as we follow the play of her mind.

VII

THE
MIND'S EYE-VIEW

PUBLICATION OF *Ulysses* IN 1922 WAS A THUNDERCLAP IN THE world of letters more resounding in its time than the thunderclap of *Madame Bovary* three quarters of a century before. Like Gustave Flaubert, James Joyce had produced a calculated work of art to which he had dedicated himself for years, with a versatility of craftsmanship far surpassing this one among his several masters. Like its predecessor, *Ulysses* was intended to astonish the world—and there is little doubt of the effect it has had upon a whole generation of writers. If Flaubert wrote into his novel his inner rage against the bourgeoisie, Joyce's work was an act of vengeance against an Ireland which (as Joyce insisted in one of his broadsides) sent its writers into banishment. In truth Joyce-Dedalus, the writer who had soared on literary wings over Europe, had banished himself, and using his own selected arms—silence, exile, cunning—had forged a complex labyrinth: forged it by the light of esthetic theories hammered out in the days of his youth. It was Joyce who, possessing an incomparable mastery of words, succeeded above all writers in capturing the atmosphere of the mind. The cunning artificer who could construct a labyrinth could also dare the labyrinth of consciousness. With him the inward turning penetrated to the deepest recesses of mental experience. He is the fountainhead of the modern psychological novel.

1

Édouard Dujardin, in his stumbling awkward way, begins *Les lauriers sont coupés* by pin-pointing the moment in the year of his novel.

> So time and place come to a point: it is the Now and Here [*c'est l'aujourd'hui, c'est l'ici*] this hour that is striking, all all around me life; the time and place, an April evening Paris. . . .

In *Ulysses*, Stephen Dedalus, mentally preparing himself for his discussion of Shakespeare in the library scene, thinks:

> Hold to the now, the here, through which all future plunges to the past.

And this recalls Bergson's "the invisible progress of the past, which gnaws into the future." Dedalus, however, has inverted the thought, and by doing so accented the present.

That moment, the Here, which becomes the past even as it is uttered or felt, is what Joyce addressed himself to catch in *Ulysses*. The modern epic, as conceived by Joyce, was originally to have been a short story in *Dubliners*. Although extended to a length far beyond anything in that volume of brief tales, it is still conceived as a moment in all time. Joyce re-created the life of an entire city in a fixed period, some eighteen hours, the date, June 16, 1904, from morning to the early hours of the next morning. He was at the same time placing this day in the history of all time, so that it becomes eighteen hours set in all the centuries, indeed in that eternity which is evoked so remarkably in one of the sermons in *A Portrait of the Artist as a Young Man*: he would create a microcosm in the cosmos, he would pick up that grain of sand which in all eternity would not even be the merest of mere fragments of the mountain. Let us listen with Dedalus to the words of the sermon in the *Portrait*:

> You have often seen the sand on the seashore. How fine are its tiny grains! And how many of those tiny little grains go to make up the small handful which a child grasps in its play. Now imagine a mountain of that sand, a million miles high, reaching from the earth to the farthest heavens, and a million miles broad, extending to remotest space, and a million miles in thickness: and imagine such an enormous mass of countless particles of sand multiplied as often as there are leaves in the forest, drops of water in the mighty ocean, feathers on birds, scales on fish, hairs on animals, atoms in the vast expanse of air: and imagine that at the end of every million years a little bird came to that mountain and carried away in its beak a tiny grain of sand. How many millions upon millions of centuries would pass before that bird had carried away even a square foot of that mountain, how many eons upon eons of ages before it had carried away all. Yet at the end of that immense stretch of time not even one instant of eternity could be said to have ended. At the end of all those billions and trillions of years eternity would have scarcely begun.

Is it any wonder that Joyce, the young artist, caught in that nightmare of time, time without end, sought to wrest a single day from it and to enclose it hard and fast in the integument of words?

This was the great frame, his subject in all its arrogant grandeur. His experiment transcended by far the first stages of the novel of subjectivity. Proust and Dorothy Richardson had confined themselves to a single consciousness. Joyce, at one leap, went far beyond them to capture the atmosphere of the mind. He not only carried his principal character forward from one volume to the next, as they had done, but he began to spin two other consciousnesses parallel to that of the young Stephen Dedalus. In addition he would give us brief glimpses into the minds of a host of other Dublin characters; Father Conmee of Clongowes who had befriended Dedalus years before; Miss Dunne, the typist, who is carrying on a correspondence with Bloom although they have never met; Master Patrick Aloysius Dignam, whose father had been buried that morning. We hear many people in this book and catch the flow of their minds; nearly always, however, we do so through other eyes—and largely through the mind's eye-view of Stephen Dedalus or Leopold Bloom.

In the multiple-scene chapter in which Joyce presents the panorama of Dublin and fills it with multiple incidents, people, minds, we become the collective eye of all the characters: for Joyce, using a technical device since much imitated, sews these scenes together with the thread of the vice-regal cavalcade that drives through the streets, ringing steel, while all the characters turn to look at the carriage. We are in Dublin—in all of it—and then always back again in the minds of Dedalus and Bloom where we see its reflection. There is much more to this strange work than the stream of consciousness of the characters: there is the Homeric frame, the literary parodies, the actual newspaper events of June 16 (that day that was to be forever after "Bloomsday" in Joyce's personal calendar). The day begins with a funeral and ends with a birth. The past disappears into the present, the future disappears into the present; both present and future become the past. And Dedalus, in the library, displaying his wit and his pedanticism explains how the artist weaves and unweaves his image in time. Past and present may be in an eternal flux; but it is possible to find a continuing point of reference:

> . . . as the mole on my right breast is where it was when I was born, though all my body has been woven of new stuff time after time, so through the ghost of the unquiet father the image of the unliving son looks forth. In the intense instant of imagination, when the mind, Shelley says, is a fading coal that which I was is that which I am and that which in possibility I may come to be. So in the future, the sister of the past, I may see myself as I sit here now but by reflection from that which then I shall be.

2

We meet Stephen Dedalus on the first page of *Ulysses*. When we enter his mind for the first time on the third page, it is to discover, in full force, the leitmotiv of his consciousness, during this particular day in Dublin. Step by step, Buck Mulligan has brought us around to it; he looks at the sea and calls it "a grey sweet mother," "our great sweet mother" and then "our mighty mother." The theme has been struck, *fortissimo*. Mulligan turns his "great searching eyes" from the sea to Stephen's face and upbraids him for his failure to kneel and pray by the bedside of his dying mother. And now Stephen's thoughts announce what will be flowing in and out of the center of his thought throughout the book.

> Stephen, an elbow rested on the jagged granite, leaned his palm against his brow and gazed at the fraying edge of his shiny black coatsleeve. Pain, that was not yet the pain of love, fretted his heart. Silently, in a dream she had come to him after her death, her wasted body within its loose brown graveclothes giving off an odour of wax and rosewood, her breath, that had bent upon him, mute, reproachful, a faint odour of wetted ashes. Across the threadbare cuffedge he saw the sea hailed as a great sweet mother by the wellfed voice beside him. The ring of bay and skyline held a dull green mass of liquid. A bowl of white china had stood beside her deathbed holding the green sluggish bile which she had torn up from her rotting liver by fits of loud groaning vomiting.

The nagging guilt, fretting at his heart, will be there all day, the "agenbite of inwit." And the word "rotting" that comes to him will run the range from decay and decomposition to putrescence. Two years have elapsed since Stephen announced in his journal, at the end of the *Portrait,* that he was going to "forge in the smithy of my soul the uncreated conscience of my race." He has not yet done this, but he will. He has lived and starved in Paris, a medical student, and memories of that residence mingle with his pre-medical studies in his reveries this June morning in Dublin:

My latin quarter hat. God, we simply must dress the character. I want puce gloves. You were a student, weren't you? Of what in the other devil's name? Paysayenn. P.C.N., you know: *physiques, chimiques et naturelles.* Aha.

He has returned hastily to Dublin summoned by telegram, to the deathbed of his mother. Now there is guilt haunting him as a nagging hurt, a fantasy, a nightmare. The prayer he refused his mother runs recurrently through his mind

Her glazing eyes, staring out of death, to shake and bend my soul. On me alone. The ghostcandle to light her agony. Ghostly light on the tortured face. Her hoarse loud breath rattling in horror, while all prayed on their knees. Her eyes on me to strike me down. *Liliata rutilantium te confessorum turma circumdet: iubilantium te virginum chorus excipiat.*
Ghoul! Chewer of corpses!
No, mother. Let me be and let me live.

Stephen is the same brilliant, arrogant, pedant-poet who gathers images from the whole reach of literature, who must tranform and parody, whose genius can abstract a whole area of reference and allusion into a phrase and whose mind must be used as an instrument of aggression against other minds. He decidedly is one who prepares a face to meet the faces that he meets, a man of brooding feeling and ashplant attitudes. A meeting with other minds is but an invitation to mental attack. "Unsheathe your dagger definitions." He will stab with definitions, with words.

—History, Stephen said, is a nightmare from which I am trying to awake.

121

From the playfield the boys raised a shout. A whirring whistle: goal. What if that nightmare gave you a back kick?
—The ways of the Creator are not our ways, Mr. Deasy said. All history moves towards one great goal, the manifestation of God.

Stephen jerked his thumb towards the window saying:
—That is God.
Hooray! Ay! Whrrhee!
—What? Mr. Deasy asked.
—A shout in the street, Stephen answered, shrugging his shoulders.

The shade of Vico presides over this conversation as A.M. Klein has brilliantly demonstrated. The shout in the street is but another manifestation of that original thunder that belonged to the Age of Gods; it is that lyric cry caught in a moment of time that rendered an emotion. But for us, in the mind of Stephen, it recalls the auditory sensibility of James Joyce, the near-sighted, for whom all Dublin is filled with shouts in the streets and voices and in whose mind the older hurt of the punishment he unjustly received at Clongowes cannot be forgotten. Mingling with the guilt-theme of his mother's death, and a series of subsidiary themes, in the dissonant symphony of Stephen's mind, filled with contrasts of beauty and ugliness, little momentary occurrences serve as reminders of what has happened long before.

In the newspaper office, to which Dedalus goes to bring a letter written by his employer, the editor lays a hand on his shoulder:

122

—I want you to write something for me, he said. Something with a bite in it. You can do it. I see it in your face. . . .

A memory is touched. The editor's words "I see it in your face . . ." belong far away to Stephen's past. He is in Clongowes Wood College again. The thought that now enters his mind is:

See it in your face. See it in your eye. Lazy idle little schemer.

The reader of *Ulysses* may wonder why Stephen thought of this. But if he has read *A Portrait of the Artist* he knows. There, Father Dolan, prefect of studies, had punished Stephen unjustly: "Out here, Dedalus. Lazy little schemer. I see schemer in your face. . . ."

A few pages later in *Ulysses* Stephen is in the library stabbing in a number of directions with his dagger definitions. "Horseness is the whatness of allhorse. . . . God: noise in the street: very peripatetic. Space: what you damn well have to see. . . ." The phrase "agenbite of inwit" comes once more into his consciousness. He thinks of himself as ever-changing and wonders whether memory still makes him the same as before when "I am other I now." He thinks of his student days, "I that sinned and prayed and fasted" and once again he soars back in time to Clongowes "A child that Conmee saved from pandies." An allusion to Father Conmee, the rector, who assured him he would not be unjustly punished again.

These allusions to the episode in the *Portrait,* brief and
fugitive, become an important episode of phantasmagoria
in the nighttown brothel scene three hundred pages farther.
Stephen lights a match but is apparently too drunk to light
his cigarette with it, for Lynch says to him: "You would
have a better chance of lighting it if you held the match
nearer." Stephen brings the match nearer to his eye and
says or thinks:

> Lynx eye. Must get glasses. Broke them yesterday. Sixteen
> years ago. Distance. The eye sees all flat. (*He draws the
> match away. It goes out.*) Brain thinks. Near: far. Ineluc-
> table modality of the visible. . . .

Clongowes and the broken glasses are again in Stephen's
mind. Memory has come rushing in and now it is sharpened
by a series of associations arising directly from external
stimuli. The cigarette slips from Stephen's fingers and he
extends his hand to the harlot, Zoë. She takes his hand and
offers to read his palm. Stephen hears or imagines her
saying, as she looks at his palm:

> "I see it in your face. The eye, like that."

And at that moment Lynch slaps Kitty's buttocks twice;
again Stephen's mind registers words either associated or
actually heard: "Like that. Pandybat."

The combination of his extended palm and a slapping
sound produce now the following images in fantasy, which
Joyce renders (as he does this entire nighttown scene) in
a mixture of speech, thought and stage directions, as if it
were a play, or rather a scenario for a film:

124

(Twice loudly a pandybat cracks, the coffin of the pianola flies open, the bald little round jack-in-the-box head of Father Dolan springs up.

FATHER DOLAN

Any boy want flogging? Broke his glasses? Lazy idle little schemer. See it in your eye.

(Mild, benign, rectorial, reproving, the head of Don John Conmee rises from the pianola coffin.)

DON JOHN CONMEE

Now, Father Dolan! Now. I'm sure that Stephen's a very good little boy.

Only those who have read *A Portrait of the Artist as a Young Man* can understand the full meaning of this fantasy as it has arisen in Stephen's intoxicated mind. The cues which brought it out of his past were the words "I see it in your face" and the sound of the two slaps administered by Lynch to Kitty. We return to Clongowes Wood College where Stephen Dedalus (in the *Portrait*) is a little boy, weak of sight. He has broken his glasses while running along the cinderpath. The prefect of studies enters the classroom and finds Stephen idle.

—Why is he not writing, Father Arnall?
—He broke his glasses, said Father Arnall, and I exempted him from work.
—Broke? What is this I hear? What is this? Your name is? said the prefect of studies.
—Dedalus, sir.
—Out here, Dedalus. Lazy little schemer. I see schemer in your face. Where did you break your glasses?
Stephen stumbled into the middle of the class, blinded by fear and haste.

125

—Where did you break your glasses? repeated the prefect of studies.

—The cinderpath, sir.

—Hoho! The cinderpath! cried the prefect of studies. I know that trick.

Stephen lifted his eyes in wonder and saw for a moment Father Dolan's whitegrey not young face, his baldy whitegrey head with fluff at the sides of it, the steel rims of his spectacles and his nocoloured eyes looking through the glasses. Why did he say he knew that trick?

—Lazy idle little loafer! cried the prefect of studies. Broke my glasses! An old schoolboy trick! Out with your hand this moment!

It is curious, however, to stumble upon other associations in Stephen's phantasmagoria in the nighttown scene which take us back not to work commonly available to the public, like the *Portrait,* but to the early fragment, *Stephen Hero,* never intended for publication by Joyce. In this fragment Stephen says to his mother:

—It is a nice thing, that you go and discuss me behind my back. Have you not your own nature to guide you, your own sense of what is right, without going to some Father Jack-in-the-box to ask him to guide you?

Here then is the explanation of Father Dolan's "jack-in-the-box" eruption from the pianola and the synthesis here, if we examine all the elements that have become fused in Stephen's mind, is that of Mother Church and the mother Stephen defied on her deathbed and the guilt he feels and cannot banish; with this also, the memory of Father Dolan with his bald round jack-in-the-box head, who administered punishment to a near-sighted guiltless boy long before at Clongowes and Stephen's years-long struggle with his waning faith. These are the tissues of past experience used by Stephen in his drunken dream-work, during a trivial episode in a Dublin bawdy house.

3

The stream of consciousness of Leopold Bloom differs markedly from that of Stephen Dedalus, inevitably, since they are two quite different personalities. The type of mind Bloom has is not unlike that of Daniel Prince in *Les lauriers sont coupés*. He sees immediate images and reflects upon them immediately; he has a literal, fact-accumulating mind. He has absorbed all kinds of data and all manner of clichés. Through him we become aware of the city, in the concrete images it flashes into his mind. We accompany him as he fusses in the kitchen to make breakfast, as he buys the pork kidney, as he attends a funeral and meanders through Dublin's streets to the newspaper office, the library, to lunch, to his encounter with the irate Citizen. After other routine adventures of daily life he and Dedalus meet, drink together and end up at the brothel.

Bloom's thoughts also have their leitmotiv. His mind keeps coming back during the day to the infidelities of his wife, to her affair with Blazes Boylan, to his own role as the cuckold. He is haunted also by the memory of his dead son, little Rudy, who died as a child and who will be identified at the end of the day with Stephen. Bloom is statistical (he is a solicitor of advertising) as we see him or his thoughts at Paddy Dignam's funeral:

Coffin now. Got here before us, dead as he is. Horse looking round at it with his plume skeowways. Dull eye: collar
tight on his neck, pressing on a bloodvessel or something.
Do they know what they cart out here every day? Must be
twenty or thirty funerals every day. Then Mount Jerome
for the protestants. Funerals all over the world everywhere
every minute. Shovelling them under by the cartload
doublequick. Thousands every hour. Too many in the
world.

He experiences a wave of anxiety as the gravediggers begin
to fill the grave.

The gravediggers took up their spades and flung heavy
clods of clay in on the coffin. Mr. Bloom turned his face.
And if he was alive all the time? Whew! By Jingo, that
would be awful! No, no: he is dead, of course. Of course
he is dead. Monday he died. They ought to have some
law to pierce the heart and make sure or an electric clock
or a telephone in the coffin and some kind of canvas air-
hole. Flag of distress. Three days. Rather long to keep them
in summer. Just as well to get shut of them as soon as you
are sure there's no.

The thought breaks here. Joyce intervenes as narrator to
write "The clay fell softer." And Bloom's thoughts resume:
"Begin to be forgotten. Out of sight, out of mind."

The worn-out phrase always serves to sum things up for
Bloom. The established phrase has a finality that his own
words cannot have. Experience for his consciousness leans
heavily on the comfort of the familiar.

Mr. Bloom walked unheeded along his grove by saddened
angels, crosses, broken pillars, family vaults, stone hopes
praying with upcast eyes, old Ireland's hearts and hands.

More sensible to spend the money on some charity for the living. Pray for the repose of the soul of. Does anybody really? Plant him and have done with him. Like down a coalshoot. Then lump them together to save time. All souls' day. . . .

From the moment he gives Marion or Molly Bloom a letter and sees her tuck it hastily under the pillow he knows that she is planning to see Blazes Boylan. All that day he tries to push this out of his mind. Little incidents however —fragments of song, a walk past a theatre, a chance remark—act as cues to force it back into the center of consciousness. Boylan has been trying to arrange a series of concerts for the musical Mrs. Bloom. Early in the book Bloom looks at the playbills outside the Queen's Theatre, a series of coming events and thinks: "He's coming in the afternoon. Her songs." Sixty pages later in Davy Byrne's, where Bloom has retreated for a sandwich, Nosey Flynn asks him about his wife's concert tour and who is getting it up. Bloom avoids answering. Then Flynn interjects: "Isn't Blazes Boylan mixed up in it?"

A warm, shock of air heat of mustard haunched on Mr. Bloom's heart. He raised his eyes and met the stare of a bilious clock. Two. Pub clock five minutes fast. Time going on. Hands moving. Two. Not yet.

In the brothel the day's little interspaced thoughts and anxieties merge into a vast fantasy of Marion and Blazes, and Bloom listens to the timepiece, sounding "Cuckoo" thrice and "the brass quoits of a bed are heard to jingle."
Stephen walks through Dublin haunted by the memory of a dead mother and his guilt. Bloom is haunted by the

129

hurt and mortification of the cuckold. He has been described as *l'homme moyen sensuel* but he has, as Lenehan remarks in the pub scene "a touch of the artist" about him. His thoughts are staccato. The immediate Dublin scene mingles with his inner wounds; and into his stream of thought come scraps of memory from the European ghettoes—for Bloom in Dublin is Odysseus the wanderer and also the Wandering Jew. And his sense of exile has its spiritual counterpart in Stephen's feeling of homelessness as an artist, even though, unlike Bloom, he is in his homeland. Stephen has spoken of Ireland as "an afterthought of Europe." The Wandering Jew can be identified also as an "afterthought"—and in the eyes of the nations, as an historic superfluity.

Bloom's mind is a pastiche of Dublin and of history. It is a rag-bag of the sentimental and the maudlin. He is alternately a functioning animal and a man with certain intellectual pretensions, yet without any curiosity. He can explain the meaning of "metempsychosis" to his illiterate wife not through any sensitivity to words but because he is a reader of "fact" magazines. He has a newspaper mind. He is gross, sensual. He loves the innards of animals; at the same time he is an affectionate man and a lover of animals.

The cat walked stiffly round a leg of the table with tail on high.
—Mkgnao!
—O, there you are, Mr Bloom said, turning from the fire.
The cat mewed in answer and stalked again stiffly round a leg of the table, mewing. Just how she stalks over my writingtable. Prr. Scratch my head. Prr.

Mr Bloom watched curiously, kindly, the lithe black form. Clean to see: the gloss of her sleek hide, the white button under the butt of her tail, the green flashing eyes. He bent down to her, his hands on his knees.

—Milk for the pussens, he said.

—Mrkgnao! the cat cried.

They call them stupid. They understand what we say better than we understand them. She understands all she wants to. Vindictive too. Wonder what I look like to her. Height of a tower? No, she can jump me.

—Afraid of the chickens she is, he said mockingly. Afraid of the chookchooks. I never saw such a stupid pussens as the pussens.

Cruel. Her nature. Curious mice never squeal. Seem to like it.

—Mrkrgnao! the cat said loudly.

She blinked up out of her avid shameclosing eyes, mewing plaintively and long, showing him her milkwhite teeth.

In the brothel scene Bloom's consciousness, like Dedalus's, is dramatized in a series of visions, a jumble of thoughts and images, described sometimes as stage directions, sometimes in speech which may not be speech so much as thought. It is written in a manner recalling Flaubert's *Temptation of St. Anthony*. Bloom fancies himself in the brothel in many roles ranging from a criminal, punished for being a cuckold, and a panderer, to the most exalted being in Europe:

A BLACKSMITH

(*Murmurs*) For the honor of God! And is that Bloom? He scarcely looks thirtyone.

A PAVIOR AND FLAGGER

That's the famous Bloom now, the world's greatest reformer. Hat's off!

(*All uncover their heads. Women whisper eagerly.*)

A MILLIONAIRESS

(*Richly*) Isn't he simply wonderful?

A NOBLEWOMAN

(*Nobly*) All that man has seen!

A FEMINIST

(*Masculinely*) And done!

A BELLHANGER

A classic face! He has the forehead of a thinker.

(*Bloom's weather. A sunburst appears in the northwest.*)

THE BISHOP OF DOWN AND CONNOR

I here present your undoubted emperor president and king chairman, the most serene and potent and very puissant ruler of this realm. God save Leopold the First!

We are now in the consciousness of Leopold the First as he begins to bestow largesse. In this scene and throughout the *Walpurgisnacht* episode, James Joyce has reached far beyond the simple straight line of thought we find in Dorothy Richardson or in *A Portrait of the Artist*. He has tried to catch—and to a marked degree has succeeded—the phantasmagoria of consciousness as well.

4

What shall we say of the stream of consciousness of Marion Tweedy Bloom, that long, rambling, unpunctuated (but paragraphed), silent monologue with which the book ends? It is perhaps no longer a stream but a torrent, a tour de force of invention and ingenuity, and certainly one of the most striking portions of the book. We have seen little of Marion Bloom during the day but have felt her presence in the continuing fantasies of her husband. In the morning

we caught a glimpse of her as Leopold served her breakfast in bed.

—What a time you were, she said.
   She set the brasses jingling as she raised herself briskly,
an elbow on the pillow. He looked calmly down on her bulk
and between her large soft bubs, sloping within her night-
dress like a shegoat's udder. The warmth of her couched
body rose on the air, mingling with the fragrance of the
tea she poured.

Then she starts searching through a book for a word she
has encountered.

—Here, she said. What does that mean?
   He leaned downward and read near her polished
thumbnail. . . .
—Metempsychosis, he said, frowning. It's Greek: from the
Greek. That means the transmigration of souls.
—O, rocks! she said. Tell us in plain words.

Molly has in this way been briefly characterized for us.
Later we glimpse only her arm, emerging from the window, as she drops a coin to a one-legged sailor during
the Dublin panorama scene. She will describe herself at
the end of the book in the language of her mind.

We enter her mind when Bloom's wanderings during
his Dublin day come to their end. He has brought Stephen
home and sobered him up. Stephen has left, and Bloom
goes to bed announcing to Molly that next morning she
must bring him his breakfast. At that moment we are introduced into her consciousness. Her thoughts come closest in
the book to what we have described as "internal monologue." Her thoughts enfold one another; involuntary asso-

ciations arise provoking others. She is in bed beside her husband and there are virtually no external stimuli to provoke their own associations. Only at one or two points do such stimuli intrude into her flow of thought: a train screeching through the night "train somewhere whistling the strength those engines have in them like big giants . . ." (Mrs. Bloom likes big strong things), then a few pages later a thought, "I can see his face clean shaven" is interrupted by "that train again." On the next page a final allusion "there's that train far away."

She seems on the whole unmindful of Bloom's presence in the bed beside her, although he is in and out of her thoughts constantly, and we gather she has been listening to him snore, for we get "O move over your big carcass out of that for the love of Mike listen to him." The state in which Joyce gives us Molly's consciousness is similar to that in which the psycho-analyst often prefers to have his patient, so that the associations may flow freely and without interruption of external stimuli—the couch, the soundless room, the supine position. We are largely in the center of Molly's thoughts, and for this reason the technique used by Joyce in this portion of *Ulysses* is less revolutionary than it seems. Only the absence of punctuation and of inhibition give the reader the sense of mental flow and of being an eyewitness to the unharnessed libido of Molly Bloom.

It is not the technique that is bold here so much as the attempt on the part of a male writer to convey the *inner* consciousness of a woman. Women writers have *described* men, and male writers women, but the description has usually been external. When Henry James wrote *The Portrait of a Lady* several women writers raised their eyebrows in surprise and one complimented him on his audacity in essaying to penetrate and convey the inner being of Isabel Archer. Dorothy Richardson's work was begun precisely because she felt that in most novels the reader moved in a male world, and she was determined to leave a record of the female consciousness. But it was Joyce who performed the creative feat of rendering Marion Tweedy Bloom almost wholly from within.

Nevertheless the question still remains whether Mrs. Bloom is not in reality a masculine concept of what the feminine mind might be and the sexuality with which Joyce endows Mrs. Bloom may have in it—particularly in its active tone—much more masculine imagination than feminine feeling. For Rebecca West at least, the fantasies of Mrs. Bloom's mind seem to lack conviction in the light of her quite satisfactory sexual encounter that afternoon with Blazes Boylan. Her accumulation of sexual daydream, much of it aggressive, would be better explained, Miss West observes, in someone undergoing "the torments of abstinence."

Such arguments simplify the problem unduly. There are in both sexes sufficient awareness of the opposite sex and components of masculinity and femininity in greater or lesser degree which enable the artist to paint men and women as they are. The question for criticism is the degree of their success. The writer of stream of consciousness has, after all, been inside no mind but his own and it is the measure of his daring that he seeks to convey the atmosphere of many other minds—Joyce that of an erotic and earthly woman, Faulkner even that of an imbecile.

5

At the end of the day in Dublin we know Stephen, Leopold and Molly more intimately than most other characters in fiction; and yet for some readers they may not be as palpable as say Becky Sharp or Emma Bovary. This might be because we have had very little chance to see Joyce's characters from the outside—to get off at a sufficient distance to take a good look at the fleshly appearance of them. Nor have we seen them together save during the brief passage in the brothel, when Stephen and Leopold meet, and the subsequent long chapter in the cabman's shelter and the chapter of catechism. There, however, they are both drunk and lost in their separate worlds. Mrs. Bloom's internal monologue is isolated at the end of the book. There is no doubt that Joyce by this means accentuates to a remarkable degree our sense of the way in which individuals move in their own envelope of consciousness, isolate and undivined. But the reader, moving with them and experiencing them, does have a picture of their lives and their lonely journeys—lonely sometimes even when most gregarious—through the world-city of Dublin.

What are the essential differences between the consciousness of Dedalus and of Bloom? The difference, markedly established, seems to me to be that between the individual who abstracts and synthesizes experience, as Stephen the poet does, and the individual who is a mere receptacle and tabulator of perceptions and sensations, registering them now blurred, now sharp, but generally passive. By this means the inner difference in the texture of the two minds is established. The minds correspond completely to the different personalities Joyce is trying to create.

Wyndham Lewis has complained that the stream-of-consciousness writer "robs work of all linear properties whatsoever, of all contour and definition . . . the romantic abdominal *within* method results in a jellyfish structure, without articulation of any sort." This judgment takes stock of the intellectual rather than emotional content of consciousness. It might be applied to some extent to Dorothy Richardson, in whose work the consciousness of Miriam is in itself the subject of the work. In *Ulysses,* where the subject is the day in Dublin, there is careful articulation and focusing of the stream of consciousness of the three principal characters. Far from being just a mass of musical notations all chords and dissonances, there is a thematic structure one might describe as symphonic which provides distinct "linear properties" over and above the Homeric frame upon which Joyce constructed his book. Stephen's thoughts take structure around his guilt-problem and Bloom's flow from the domestic situation in Eccles Street.

The musical structure of *Ulysses* and the music of *Finnegans Wake* take us back not only to Joyce's own musical training and his aural sensitivity—he had hoped to become a professional singer—but again to the theories of the symbolists. Dujardin always said that Wagner was the main source of inspiration for the internal monologue in

Les lauriers sont coupés, equating the themes which the mind calls up recurrently in the form of memories with the flowing Wagnerian label-themes.

One of the most illuminating episodes of Joyce's middle years was his espousal in Paris of the cause of his fellow countryman, the tenor Sullivan. The Irish singer had difficulty obtaining bookings at the Paris Opera, although he was the the only singer then available who could reach all the high notes in *William Tell* and *Les Huguenots*, operas that were being revived that year. Whenever Sullivan did get a chance to appear, Joyce led a claque to the opera. His "bravo, bravo" seemed to hit the great chandelier and, echoing through the opera house, was the signal for applause. "Sullivan sings 45 G's, 93 A flats, 92 A's, 54 B flats, 15 B's, 19 C's and two C sharps," Joyce exulted after examining the score of *William Tell*. The novelist was offering statistics in the manner of Leopold Bloom: but it was also Joyce, the Irish tenor, who had become a writer instead of a singer, admiring the performance of a fellow-virtuoso. Since thoughts repeat themselves in different forms and recur at irregular intervals, unpredictable and involuntary, by a process of association, they constituted themselves for James Joyce as the recurring notes of a musical score, a kind of music of the mind. Memorable in *Ulysses* is the long chapter written in fugal structure, set in Ormond's Bar, where the themes enunciated at the beginning are developed note by note amid the drinking, the hubbub, the clinking of glasses, the sounds and voices and snatches of song, while bronze by gold, Miss Douce's head by Miss Kennedy's, the barmaids, float in and out of sound, two islands of color.

From the moment the artist attempts to render the music of the mind, the counterpoint of consciousness, as Joyce did, he is caught up as we have seen in the Here and the Now "through which all future plunges to the past." Consciousness, however, does not measure time by mechanical means. It possesses its own time measure, different within each individual. The psychological novelist must actively concern himself, accordingly, with psychological time.

VIII

THE ARBITRARY DIAL: EPIPHANY

THE NOVELS WE HAVE BEEN DISCUSSING HAVE BEEN CALLED BY some critics "time-novels." Certainly *time* might be said to be their primary concern. We have seen how in *Ulysses* Joyce was preoccupied with the preservation, in words, of eighteen hours of experience, retrieved so to speak from all eternity. So Marcel Proust's quest for "lost time" is an attempt on an heroic scale to recapture the memories of moments that have long disappeared but which still live somewhere in the consciousness. These too may be preserved in an enduring mould of words. Proust spoke of his wish to "seize, isolate, immobilize for the duration of a lightning flash . . . a fragment of pure time in its pure state." Dostoevsky expressed an analogous wish when he described the heightening of sensory experience—the "aura"—just before an epileptic seizure and remarked that he would have given years of his life to live through a few such moments gathered together and made continuous. Virginia Woolf recurs constantly to "the moment" which, like Blake's grain of sand, can hold a world within its fractional pulse—the very incandescence of consciousness. And William Faulkner, coming after these explorers, wrote into the core of his work the meaning of the "arbitrary dial," whose shadow marks the Present and absorbs also all that is Past.

The face of the mechanical clock stares at us from these novels: we hear the hours ticking, bells ring, clocks chime, Big Ben's bronze syllables float through the London air, and in the Dublin of Joyce's discarded fragment, *Stephen Hero*, young Dedalus looks upon the face of the clock and experiences—an epiphany!

> He told Cranly that the clock of the Ballast Office was capable of an epiphany. Cranly questioned the inscrutable dial of the Ballast Office with his no less inscrutable countenance:
> —Yes, said Stephen, I will pass it time after time, allude to it, refer to it, catch a glimpse of it. It is only an item in the catalogue of Dublin's street furniture. Then all at once I see it and I know at once what it is: epiphany.
> —What?
> —Imagine my glimpse at that clock as the gropings of a spiritual eye which seeks to adjust its vision to an exact focus. The moment the focus is reached the object is epiphanised.

By an "epiphany" he meant "a sudden spiritual manifestation, whether, in the vulgarity of speech or in a memorable phrase of the mind itself." And the young Dedalus believed that "it was for the man of letters to record these epiphanies with extreme care seeing that they themselves are the most delicate and evanescent of moments." Although Joyce discarded the term in the final form of the *Portrait*, he defines very carefully in that book—with the aid of St. Thomas Aquinas—the esthetic experience implicit in his concept of the artist's epiphany: isolation of the given image from its surroundings—*integritas*; perception of formal harmony in it—*consonantia;* and the emotional content of the experience—*claritas*. The process is often simultaneous, in an instant of perception, that instant when "the clear radiance of the aesthetic image is apprehended luminously by the mind which has been arrested by its wholeness and fascinated by its harmony." In this lies the "silent stasis of aesthetic pleasure," Joyce visioned as a spiritual state (hence the original term "epiphany"), what Galvani called the "enchantment of the heart."

Joyce here is describing in reality the functioning of the creative imagination: what occurs in an artist's mind before he begins the difficult act of recording and communicating his experience. The novelist was aware, however, that much of what he imaginatively experienced could be recorded only in the most approximate way, by use of symbols, and that what would be communicated—if anything —might be largely an atmosphere and a state of feeling, as complex and subjective in the reader as in the experience of the writer. When Joyce described Verlaine's poems as "remote from conscious purpose as rain that falls in a garden . . . the rhythmic speech of an emotion otherwise incommunicable," he was suggesting—with the symbolists —that in literature words and symbols alone can communicate, in the most general fashion and largely atmospherically, emotions that otherwise defy both rendering and communication. Stephen Dedalus asks himself: "Did he then love the rhythmic rise and fall of words better than their associations of legend and colour?" Joyce, as the world was to discover, began by loving words in this way

145

but ultimately sought to make them convey the legends and associations they symbolized, as well as the colors and tones they suggested, to his imagination. Sounds, words, like thoughts, are experienced in time and they have been, from primitive days man's means of giving vocal expression to emotion.

> The lyrical form is in fact the simplest verbal vesture of an instant of emotion, a rhythmical cry such as ages ago cheered on the man who pulled at the oar or dragged stones up a slope. He who utters it is more conscious of the instant of emotion than of himself as feeling emotion.

Finnegans Wake is already upon the horizon. While Joyce seized upon the visual, the palpable in experience, he sought, with perhaps the most sensitive ear in English literature since Shakespeare and Milton, to render that which was audible as well. Stephen at one moment in *Ulysses* equates a shout in the street with God, thus suggesting the spiritual qualities Joyce felt in this synthesis by which the audible or the visible or both—time or space or again both—merge in the artist's consciousness to form his "instant of emotion" or epiphany.

The psychological novelist attempts to arrest a moment of time at every step even as it flees before him. He may contemplate a statue, a picture, a landscape, a city, for hours: always the form of what is being viewed remains reasonably fixed and recognizable. But the instant of emotion, the moment of perception, the shout in the street, the epiphany—these are heard and are gone, the moment flames brightly and becomes a fading coal. How arrest this kinetic moment of the mind? How give it the static

146

quality possessed by a statue? This was at the heart of Joyce's problem—and the problem of those who followed in his footsteps. When she was at work on *To the Lighthouse* Virginia Woolf set down these lines in her diary:

> . . . I am now and then haunted by some semi-mystic very profound life of a woman, which shall all be told on one occasion; and time shall be utterly obliterated; future shall somehow blossom out of the past. One incident—say the fall of a flower—might contain it. My theory being that the actual event practically does not exist—nor time either. . . .

The "slice of life" of the nineteenth century realists here becomes the "slice of time." From trying to capture "the moment"—say the fall of a flower—the artist begins to question whether the moment ever existed. Only he knows that it does exist—as a kind of eternal present.

2

This intense awareness of time as a merging of time past and time present, as T. S. Eliot has put it,

> Time past and time future
> What might have been and what has been
> Point to one end, which is always present . . .

is at the very core of the work of William Faulkner. Proust's awareness resided in his aching need to recover the past; Faulkner's arose from his having grown up in a society in which the past had virtually engulfed the present. A South in which the Civil War exists as a contemporary reality in the minds of young men who listen largely to talk of the Long Before; in which animosities have never

been extinguished and old feelings continue to bubble and
to rage, is very like Faulkner's Benjy who has been three
years old for thirty years. There is no dividing line between
what is and what was in Benjy's retarded consciousness, no
distinction between an immediate reality and memory.
Reverend Hightower, preaching fervently to his flock,
could still hear the clatter of horses' hooves and see the
great swirl of dust of the old war, although he was born
after the struggle; and Sam Fathers, telling young McCas-
lin stories of a family past, made them seem in the present:

> And as he talked about those old times and those dead
> and vanished men of another race from either that the boy
> knew, gradually to the boy those old times would cease
> to be old times and would become a part of the boy's pres-
> ent, not only as if they had happened yesterday but as if
> they were still happening, the men who walked through
> them actually walking in breath and air and casting an
> actual shadow on the earth they had not quitted.

William Faulkner, who had been transported from the
New World to the Old as an aviator of the First World
War, had ample opportunity to observe this strange process: in Oxford, Mississippi, he had become aware of the
melting together of the Old South and the New and seen
how legends persist long after their creators are gone. By
a coincidence, he was stationed at Oxford, England. For
him the two Oxfords, each encased in its own long tradition, could melt together even as the American recovers in
England certain elements of his own past and present.
Indeed the new war could melt into the old. And so, too,
the story of Calvary had become timeless and had been

enacted anew, while being a repetition of what had happened before.

The structure and content of Faulkner's masterpiece, *The Sound and the Fury*, can be understood only if we grasp his singular absorption with time—or timelessness. On the surface it appears to be a story of the three Compson sons, told to us through their stream of consciousness on three different days. In this process, however, we become acquainted with the decay of the Compson family, and by the same token of the American South. We observe, and are made to feel, the swallowing up of the present by the past.

As Cranly, in Joyce's fragment, questions "the inscrutable dial of the Ballast Office," Quentin Compson questions the "round stupid assertion of the clock." He, however, wants to wipe it out of existence. If time could stand still he would not have to die. Having fixed the hour for his suicide, he can live only by annihilating time. He tears the hands off his father's watch (which was also his grandfather's) but the ticking does not cease. (So the South had torn the hands of time without shutting out its inexorable tick.) His father had told him that clocks slay time and had given him the ancestral watch "not that you may remember time, but that you might forget it now and then for a moment, and not spend all your breath trying to conquer it." Nevertheless Quentin spends the last day of his life in a kind of time-rage trying to conquer it. In tearing the hands off the watch he seeks to obliterate the present. Obliteration of the present, however, is a denial of life.

And life refuses to be denied. The sun pursues its course,

149

shadows lengthen, time-whistles blow, the "staring eyes" of clocks are encountered. These may be contradictory and confusing, as Quentin, leaving the jewelry store, discovers:

> I went out, shutting the door upon the ticking. I looked back into the window. . . . There were about a dozen watches in the window, a dozen different hours and each with the same assertive and contradictory assurance that mine had, without any hands at all. Contradicting one another. I could hear mine, ticking away inside my pocket, even though nobody could see it, even though it could tell nothing if anyone could.

But it ticks on to sunset. The day does have an ending. So Quentin destroys himself, in reality because he has been unable to put the present into meaningful relation with the past.

Jason, the Compson who seems at first glance to be completely in touch with reality, deploys a vast surface energy in acting out his hatred of his fellow men and in hoarding petty sums. His father had urged his sons not to "spend all your breath" trying to conquer time. Jason is always breathless. He knows only mechanical time; he runs in his little maze and cannot stop running. He is nearly always late and all the while he strains to be on time. His time-sense is as faulty as Quentin's, but at the opposite extreme. He knows only the inching present, as Quentin knew only an engulfing past. All he achieves is a constant self-frustration. The present has trapped him in a chamber a few city blocks long. As Quentin sought to forget the present, so Jason is incapable of forgetting it. Time for both is an unsorted jumble. . . .*

We have already alluded to Benjy, the third Compson, for whom time has no boundaries and whose imbecile consciousness remembers only by blurred associations: he is thirty-three at one moment, thirteen at another. And suddenly he is a boy of five. Experience is all one, names and places cannot be distinguished from one another, the entire world moves around him comfortable when familiar, anxiety-provoking when unfamiliar. He can hear the dark; the spoon "came up and I ate" and "the bowl steamed up to my face." The lawn comes to him and goes away. Benjy lives in a world of presence and absence, of immediate sensations that are also past sensations. Faulkner has created him in a vein of compassionate poetry, making of him a kind of repository of all the emotional chaos of the Compsons.

In the Compson household only one person has a firm grip on time and, by this token, on reality. This is Dilsey, the Negro cook. She is aware that the clock of the South lags. She knows that for the Negro in the South there is always a difference in time. To the chiming of the Compson family clock she listens attentively. She counts its hours. Then she adds three more.

Faulkner boldly violated chronological sequence in *The Sound and the Fury*, perhaps in imitation of the human consciousness itself. The mind cannot accommodate itself

* See Perrin Lowrey's admirable discussion of this in "Concepts of Time in *The Sound and the Fury*," in *English Institute Essays* (N.Y. 1954).

to chronological or mechanical time, but is constantly moving blocks of time from past-to-present-to-past, and without regard for logical sequence. In doing this the American novelist showed how completely he had grasped the essential characteristic of the psychological novel. The time of the book covers only four days—the three days of the three brothers plus Dilsey's day—yet it covers the entire emotional history of the Compson family (which is also the emotional history of the South). We are in Benjy's mind on April 7, 1928. We are in Quentin Compson's mind, during the second section, eighteen years *earlier*, June 2, 1910, the day he drowned himself. We are in Jason Compson's mind April 6, 1928, the day *before* we were in Benjy's mind. And in the final section the omniscient author returns to the scene to tell us in conventional fashion the events of April 8, 1928, Dilsey's day—the day *after* the Benjy section. Only when we have read the entire book is it possible to unscramble the time element and allow all the data to fall into place in our mind. The problems involved in reading *The Sound and the Fury* are not unlike those discussed earlier in connection with Dorothy Richardson, with this significant difference: in Miss Richardson's work we were sorting out the data furnished us by one mind, whereas here we have, by the end of the book, lived through three highly dissimilar minds and discovered how they were related to a common family experience. In making us aware of the disordered time-sense of real life, that is of psychological time, Faulkner not only dramatized for us the three minds and the confusion of time that exists in memory, but heightened our awareness of the depths of mental experience. At the same time his book serves to dramatize the fact that when a novelist takes us into the minds of his characters he can no longer remain in an historical past, seeking out for us a story of what *has* happened. He must confront us with what *is* happening at the very moment that Quentin is smashing the face of his father's watch, or Big Ben is chiming 11 a.m. for Mrs. Dalloway or the clocks in Oxford Street are pointing to 1.30 p.m. for Hugh Whitbread. And this points to the larger goal of the psychological novelist, exemplified in Proust and his search for time past and "pure time"—his sense that the chiming and ticking are constant reminders of an ebbing time in a consciousness that in reality lives only in a momentary present, an endless past. This larger goal is to enshrine experience and thereby render it impervious to time.

The accretion of historical and geographical memory that the two Oxfords symbolize in the biography of William Faulkner—evident to a marked degree in his retelling as a fable for our time of the Christ story—was what James Joyce tried to record in a different way in *Ulysses* and *Finnegans Wake*. Each in their own way, the Irish writer and the American who followed him, arrived at a vision of mental experience as something overlaid with a multitude of meanings, and each crystallized in his art the richness of that experience.

In *Ulysses* Joyce had demonstrated how the seemingly "jellyfish" material of consciousness could be used to expand one of his epiphanies into a great picture of a single day in a teeming city. In *The Sound and the Fury*, by taking us into three minds, Faulkner made us aware of the tragedy of the South. In both these works the streams of consciousness were poured into a series of moulds; yet for all their moulding, the thoughts and sensations of each consciousness portrayed had to be assimilated by the consciousness of the reader. The interesting critical problem that we may now formulate is this: however ingenious and however different the portrayal of the three streams of consciousness in *Ulysses* and in *The Sound and the Fury*, they each spring in reality from a single stream of consciousness, that is the mind and being of James Joyce or William Faulkner. In other words: Is the creation of offshoots of a consciousness—however rich the off-shoots—in essence a form of autobiography, the emptying of the artist's mind to artistic ends? This is the all-but-final step in our inquiry.

IX

THE NOVEL AS AUTOBIOGRAPHY

In *Honeycomb,* THE THIRD CHAPTER OR VOLUME OF HER *Pilgrimage,* Dorothy Richardson's heroine, Miriam Henderson, makes a discovery while she is reading a book. It is that "I don't read books for the story, but as a psychological study of the author." Books come to mean to her "not the people in the books, but knowing, absolutely, everything about the author. . . . In life everything was so scrappy and mixed up. In a book the author was there in every word."

She embroiders this. "If only she could make Eve see what a book was . . . a dance by the author, a song, a prayer, an important sermon, a message. Books were not stories printed on paper, they were people; the real people. . . ."

In Virginia Woolf's early novel, *The Voyage Out,* a character talking about his unwritten novels says, "All you read a novel for is to see what sort of person the writer is, and, if you know him, which of his friends he's put in. As for the novel itself, the whole conception, the way one's seen the thing, felt about it, made it stand in relation to other things, not one in a million cares for that."

Criticism of course does care. And the problem that

157

arises, particularly in the psychological novel, is whether we do not have so much more of the writer than in the conventional novel—since he has, so to speak, emptied the contents of his inner self for us. "The danger," wrote Virginia Woolf in her diary in 1920, "is the damned egotistical self; which ruins Joyce and Richardson to my mind: is one pliant and rich enough to provide a wall for the book from oneself without its becoming, as in Joyce and Richardson, narrowing and restricting?" She was writing, of course, before she had read all of *Ulysses*. But the problem she stated was concrete enough. Does the psychological novelist write *fiction*, in the fullest sense of the word, or the book of himself? Is it possible to provide the "wall for the book from oneself" that Virginia Woolf would have liked to erect?

1

During the last year of his life Marcel Proust was asked by the journal *Les Annales* to discuss the distinction between the analytical novel and the adventure novel. He replied that the expression "analytical novel" was not to his taste. It had come to mean, he said, a study under a microscope, and he added "the instrument I prefer is the telescope." He went on:

> . . . I was unfortunate enough to start a book with the word, "I," and immediately it was assumed that instead of trying to discover universal laws, I was "analysing myself," in the personal and odious sense of the word. I shall, therefore, if you are willing, replace the term "analytical novel" by "introspective novel."

158

After discussing adventure novels, he went on to say that the introspective novel must not be a novel of pure intellect.

> It has to do with drawing a reality out of the unconscious in such a way as to make it enter into the realm of the intellect, while trying to preserve its life, not to garble it, to subject it to the least possible shrinkage—a reality which the light of intellect alone would be enough to destroy, so it seems. To succeed in this work of salvage, all the forces of the mind and even of the body, are not superfluous. It is a little like the cautious, docile, intrepid effort necessary to someone who, while still asleep, would like to explore his sleep with his mind without this intervention leading to his awakening. His precautions must be taken. But although it apparently embodies a contradiction, this form of work is not impossible.

It *was* possible. Proust himself demonstrated this, as the sixteen volumes published by Gallimard show. What Proust is saying about trying to discover the nature of sleep without waking up is akin to what William James said when he spoke of turning up the gas to discover what the darkness is like. Proust believed, however, that in that fragment of a fragment of a second, in which the gas begins to cast its light into the darkness, the precious moment of pure time can be caught in static form. How difficult that is, we may judge from the fact that it took all of Proust's energies and his whole life to arrive at a few such fragments of experience, and this by the process not of the *immediate* capturing and recording of the epiphany, but by the slow, deep, search of memory through film upon film of association.

159

It may seem whimsical and perverse for a novelist as addicted to analyzing a moment as we would analyze a year, to invoke the telescope rather than the microscope. Yet Proust was being perfectly honest. His purpose, as we know, was a search for universal laws, for Time—not the time which we see ticking its way mechanically across the face of a clock, but that Time which sometimes makes five minutes seem like a day and makes a day sometimes pass as if it were five minutes.

Henry James, sitting down to write the first volume of his memoirs, *A Small Boy and Others,* used a phrase on the very first page that showed him—engaged as he was in the process of writing autobiography—to be starting with the same essential purpose as Proust (and it was at the same time, also, for James's first volume was published in 1913, the year of *Swann's Way*). He speaks on the first page of "my interrogation of the past." This could be a way of freely translating *À la recherche du temps perdu.* "It was to memory in the first place," said James, "that my main appeal for particulars had to be made."

We have thus exemplified here, in the one case in an autobiography and in the other in a novel that appears to be thinly disguised autobiography, the working of the same process. Memory and association—the word "association" flowers on page after page of James's memoirs—are the primary source of autobiography as they are of fiction. This, however, is a very bald and quite unsubtle statement of a matter infinitely complex.

To understand better the relationship between autobiography and the novel let us look briefly into the texture of the memories invoked by the two writers. Here is a small boy remembering his love of the theatre:

> Every morning I would hasten to the Moriss column to see what new plays it announced. Nothing could be more disinterested or happier than the dreams with which these announcements filled my mind, dreams which took their form from the inevitable associations of the words forming the title of the play, and also from the colour of the bills, still damp and wrinkled with paste, on which those words stood out. Nothing, unless it were such strange titles as the *Testament de César Girodot* or *Œdipe-Roi,* inscribed not on the green bills of the Opéra-Comique, but on the wine-coloured bills of the Comédie-Française, nothing seemed to me to differ more profoundly from the sparkling white plume of the *Diamants de la Couronne* than the sleek, mysterious satin of the *Domino Noir.* . . .

And here is another small boy remembering:

> . . . there were finer vibrations as well—for the safely-prowling infant, though none perhaps so fine as when he stood long and drank deep at those founts of romance that gushed from the huge placards of the theatre. These announcements, at a day when advertisement was contentedly but information, had very much the form of magnified play-bills; they consisted of vast oblong sheets, yellow or white, pasted upon tall wooden screens or into hollow sockets, and acquainting the possible playgoer with every circumstance that might seriously interest him. These screens rested sociably against trees and lamp-posts as well as against walls and fences, to all of which they were, I suppose, familiarly attached; but the sweetest note of their confidence was that, in parallel lines and the good old way, characters facing performers, they gave the whole cast, which in the "palmy days" of the drama often involved

161

many names. I catch myself again in the fact of endless stations in Fifth Avenue near the south-west corner of Ninth Street, as I think it must have been, since the dull long "run" didn't exist then for the young *badaud* and the poster there was constantly and bravely renewed. It engaged my attention, whenever I passed, as the canvas of a great master in a great gallery holds that of the pious tourist, and even though I can't at this day be sure of its special reference I was with precocious passion "at home" among the theatres. . . .

The seventy-year-old man remembering the precocious passion of the small boy in New York for the theatre was perhaps less addicted to searching for the finer mental *odor* of his experience than the middle-aged man in the cork-lined room looking at his boyhood self before the playbills of the Théâtre Français. Yet both were writing curiously similar autobiography and each for a different end. In the case of Henry James it was for the pleasure of studying the growth of an imagination, *his* imagination. In the case of Proust it was to carry out a process of remembering, to discover the very nature of memory. Nevertheless there are many significant parallels to be discerned in these dissimilar works. Perhaps this shows how similar the interests and awarenesses of small sensitive boys may be even in cultures and cities as removed from each other and as different as New York and Paris:

. . . upon the permanent foundation of eggs, cutlets, potatoes, preserves, and biscuits, whose appearance on the table she no longer announced to us, Françoise would add —as the labour of fields and orchards, the harvest of the tides, the luck of the markets, the kindness of neighbours, and her own genius might provide; and so effectively that our bill of fare, like the quatrefoils that were carved on the porches of cathedrals in the thirteenth century, reflected to some extent the march of the seasons and the incidents of human life—a brill, because the fish-woman had guaranteed its freshness; a turkey, because she had seen a beauty in the market at Roussainville-le-Pin; cardoons with marrow, because she had never done them for us in that way before; a roast leg of mutton, because the fresh air made one hungry and there would be plenty of time for it to 'settle down' in the seven hours before dinner; spinach, by way of a change; apricots, because they were still hard to get; gooseberries, because in another fortnight there would be none left; raspberries, which M. Swann had brought specially; cherries, the first to come from the cherry-tree, which had yielded none for the last two years; a cream cheese, of which in those days I was extremely fond; an almond cake, because she had ordered one the evening before; a fancy loaf, because it was our turn to 'offer' the holy bread. And when all these had been eaten, a work composed expressly for ourselves, but dedicated more particularly to my father, who had a fondness for such things, a cream of chocolate, inspired in the mind, created by the hand of Françoise, would be laid before us, light and fleeting as an 'occasional piece' of music, into which she had poured the whole of her talent.

The boy in New York did not have as refined a palate. Nothing as fine as the *omelette aux tomates* and bottle of straw-colored Chablis that Lambert Strether and Madame de Vionnet consume in *The Ambassadors*, is evoked in *A Small Boy and Others*. The memories, nevertheless, are of a distinctly American palate, ice cream consumed at every turn, hot cakes and sausages flooded with molasses on the hospitable porch of some Southern neighbors who settled in Fourteenth Street, doughnuts on Broadway, and waffles by the hundreds "the oblong farinaceous compound, faintly yet richly brown, stamped and smoking, not crisp nor brittle, but softly absorbent of the syrup dabbed upon it" and then peaches! Ah, the peaches *d'antan!* The small boy remembered certain "capital peach trees" in his grand-mother's back yard in Albany and peaches on the New York waterfront

> . . . bushels of peaches in particular, peaches big and peaches small, peaches white and peaches yellow, played a part in life from which they have somehow been deposed; every garden, almost every bush and the very boys' pockets grew them; they were "cut up" and eaten with cream at every meal; domestically "brandied" they figured, the rest of the year, scarce less freely—if they were rather a "party dish" it was because they made the party whenever they appeared, and when ice-cream was added, or they were added *to* it, they formed the highest revel we knew. Above all the public heaps of them, the high-piled receptacles at every turn, touched the street as with a sort of southern plenty. . . . We ate everything in those days by the bushel and the barrel, as from stores that were infinite. . . .

The two passages illustrate in a rather striking fashion the workings of memory in one artist to the end of autobi-ography and the workings of memory in another artist to the subtler end of fiction. The common ground on which both stand is in their attempt to render the truth of experi-ence. The Proustian food is not mere enumeration, mingled with a kind of smacking of the lips that one senses in the Jamesian memories; in each case each item matches the season, the occasion, the opportunity, and each season, occasion and opportunity is the rationale of Françoise's choice; so that what has been evoked in the Proustian autobiography that is fiction, as distinct from the Jamesian autobiography that is autobiography, is also a subtle and rather wonderful characterization of Françoise—the brill, "because she had seen a beauty in the market," the roast mutton, "because the fresh air made one hungry and there would be plenty of time for it to 'settle down' in the seven hours before dinner" and so on.

What this can be held to demonstrate is that fiction can be autobiographical, but that this does not mean that it is autobiography. And while this may seem a truism, it must be stated so that we may attempt to determine the extent to which a work can be dissociated from the life that produces it.

2

Proceeding in this empirical fashion, let us now glance briefly at two works which have been fortuitously preserved. They were discarded by their authors who, in the very process of writing them, were making certain important discoveries about their art—and about themselves— discoveries indeed that prompted them to set aside these early attempts. They had outlived their usefulness even before completion. The first is the fragment, *Stephen Hero*, which consists of the materials Joyce finally worked into the last chapter of *A Portrait of the Artist as a Young Man*, but which is almost as long as the final novel. The second is the 300,000-word incomplete novel, *Jean Santeuil* (incomplete, though it is the equivalent of at least three modern-length novels). This was discovered among Proust's papers and was published in three volumes with a preface by André Maurois. [It has not yet been translated into English.] Chance thus has provided us with a glimpse into two autobiographical novels, both in their primitive and almost wholly autobiographical state. This is a remarkable stroke of fortune for criticism. We are given an opportunity to see the artists making their false starts, recognizing their mistakes, and consciously rectifying them.

In both cases these—shall we call them preliminary?—works are remarkable, as they well might be, given the pens that wrote them. *Jean Santeuil,* which, for all its incompleteness, it is difficult to speak of as a fragment, stands as a beautifully written and very finely *felt* work that would have placed Proust high in the ranks of twentieth century French writers even if he had written nothing else. *Stephen Hero,* this more truly a fragment, has much of the Joycean verbal magic even if it is without the virtuoso touches of the novelist's later writing. Both are derived out of the daily lives of their authors. Joyce indeed spoke of the *Portrait* or *Stephen Hero* as his "autobiographical" novel in a letter to his publisher. Proust sought to conceal the autobiography behind an elaborate prologue quite in the manner of Henry James. He turned himself into a first-person narrator who listens to the novel *Jean Santeuil* as it is read aloud by a great novelist during their stay in a farmhouse in Britanny. A little preface of three sentences admits that the work is autobiographical, except that we are supposed to regard this as the preface of the novelist in the story, not of Proust the young listener and admirer:

> May I call this book a novel? It is less than a novel and perhaps much more, the very essence of my life, gathered with nothing added to it, in those hours of laceration in which it was lived. This book was never created; it was harvested. [*Ce livre n'a jamais été fait, il a été récolté.*]

And André Maurois, one of Proust's biographers and critics, confirms that *Jean Santeuil* is very close to Proust's own life. In the novel's opening pages we discover the episode of the good-night kiss that will color the launching of the mind's drama in *Swann's Way*; a childish episode with a girl named Marie forecasts the story of Gilberte. The Proust parents (still alive when this was written in the late 1890's) are drawn in greater detail, apparently from life. Bergotte is there, but as painter rather than writer. There is a direct presentation of the tumult of emotion aroused by the Dreyfus case that will be treated later in much more indirect fashion. The *petite phrase* is clearly from a work by Saint-Saëns. The theme of homosexuality appears, but faintly. The central portion of the book shows Jean in society and much of this is painted from the same palette as the later work. The lilacs bloom, perhaps with a less delicate odor. The book is the work of a Proust who has not yet discovered Ruskin. There is no Swann, and no Charlus but—and this is extremely important—there are incidents in Jean's life which will later be incorporated into the life of Swann. At moments Proust is near his later search for involuntary memory, but it is not yet quite that; rather it is memory transposed into a direct and felt immediate reality. The haunting and poetic unity of the later work is here in an attentuated form. What we have is directness and freshness. We catch Proust in the process of his development and writing autobiography—the memoir in the form of a novel.

So in *Stephen Hero* certain of the fully developed scenes will later be treated in an indirect fashion or be dropped altogether. Joyce's first style is simple, matter-of-fact, frugal; and there is a bareness in the catalogue of Stephen's feelings and doings at the university which is in striking contrast to the work that emerged from it. The incident of Joyce's paper on "Drama and Life" and his proposal to Emma that she become his mistress, which stands out here as evidence of Stephen's juvenility, are later pushed aside. What we get largely is a picture of an aggressive young artist, suffering from a constant need to assert himself in his drab surroundings and in a life he finds stifling. He is defending himself against the world at every turn. This he does by a cold intellectualism, an eloquence that borders on constant speech-making, a search for the esoteric in scholarship and the assumption of an attitude defiant and arrogant.

In this fragment we are given Stephen's theory of art much as it was to be enunciated in *A Portrait of the Artist,* but it is here broken up among other episodes and its exposition lacks the unity and coherence it will have later. In the successor work the statement on art marks Stephen's arrival at intellectual maturity. Once he has defined a theory of art, he is at the end of his youth. The artist as a young man may go out into the world and begin to fashion his work.

One element in the esthetics of *Stephen Hero* is omitted from the *Portrait*. This is the theory of the epiphany. Joyce dropped this from the early draft, almost as if it were a private device, a personal matter. He alludes to it only later, in passing, in *Ulysses* and in terms that show he considered it as belonging to his nonage:

Remember your epiphanies on green oval leaves, deeply deep, copies to be sent if you died to all the great libraries of the world, including Alexandria?

Like *Jean Santeuil, Stephen Hero* has freshness and directness, an acuteness of observation and sharpness of style that makes us regret that more of it was not preserved when, so the story runs, Nora Joyce snatched it from the fire into which her husband threw it.

What the two artists did when they discarded these earlier works and started afresh was curiously similar. Proust rewrote *Jean Santeuil* into a first-person novel in which we are almost wholly in the narrator's mind. Having tried to be scrupulously objective (and having utilized the mechanism of a story within a story, and a narrator) he now candidly gave his novel an autobiographical cast. We may speculate that the death of his parents made the earlier reticences unnecessary; and the development of his process of self-examination through accretion of reverie and memory made the first person the only *truthful* way in which the self-examination could be reported without having to go through the technical difficulties involved in transferring this to another consciousness. Joyce, in both the early version and the final form of the *Portrait*, maintained the third person, but he turned a narrative wholly

169

objective into one wholly subjective. In both cases the rewriting was in pursuit of subjective experience: a need to look into the mind, inward that is, as well as outward from the mind at the world.

In a sense, therefore, these novels became more deeply autobiographical than before. Yet in another sense, they were farther removed from autobiography for, as we have seen, that which was Proust's biography now became part of the biography of Swann, even as the mind of Joyce, creating the mind of Stephen, in due course was to father Leopold and Molly Bloom. It is at this point, therefore, that we can profitably try to refine the question of the relationship between autobiography and the psychological novel.

3

In a broad sense, that is in a general psychological sense, everything we do is an expression of ourselves. How we walk and how we talk, the nervous impulses that drive our pen across a sheet and give an individual form to our handwriting, the words we speak and the phrases and sentences we build out of them, the images we conjure up and the objects our eyes select, these are all autobiographical acts, so that a book that we write is the book of ourselves. When a poet writes the simplest lyric his choice of word and image and symbol is *his* and no one else's; and if he is guilty of plagiarism he has still made a choice in cribbing from one writer rather than from another. It is still a self-revealing act. In a world of multiple choices there is always a reason, although it may be obscure, why one choice is made rather than another. And it is on this ground that criticism, which seeks to discover the quality of the mind that produced a given work, has every reason to invoke the aid of the biographer. Indeed the passion to discover the mind behind the work as well as the mind *in* the work explains why, failing to find the man Shakespeare, a whole school of speculation has discovered a compelling need to create another man. Perhaps all this is another way of saying that the style is the man. But it means also that the man is the style; that fragments of experience of the man have been moulded to produce the art and that if we knew enough about any artist we could redissolve his art and find in it the biographical ingredients that shaped it. This would certainly be the case with the psychological novelist, even more than with the conventional novelist, since he gives us access to his mind.

The three main streams of consciousness in *Ulysses* spring from a single source; however different each may be, they are tributaries of the central stream of consciousness that feeds them. This central stream was the mind of James Joyce. The question which we must ask, therefore, is this: Is not a novel using stream-of-consciousness devices by its very nature an autobiographical novel? Does not such a novel tell us a great deal more than most novels about the mind of its writer? Are we not being given the very texture of the writer's experience and the very atmosphere of *his* mind? In a word, is not stream-of-consciousness writing another form of memoir-writing, that is a recapturing of the past of the writer, as if he had decided to write his memoirs? Is he not shuffling associations and memories

171

in the pretense that they are fiction, or transferring them to characters (really disguises of himself) to create the impression that they belong to someone else? And if that be the case, what difference is there between memoirs such as Saint-Simon's and a novel of Proust's? Was not Casanova, in setting down his adventures, writing memoirs of his overactive life as fact just as Proust was writing the memoirs of his overactive mind as fiction?

If we accept this line of argument, then we must agree that Marcel Proust wrote autobiography and not a novel, since he was forever reaching into his own mind and re-creating his own past in his search for the truths of experience. And yet Proust—who went so far as to call his hero Marcel—was the first to deny over and over again that he was writing autobiographical fiction. He was constantly asked about the persons he had put into his novel; and he constantly replied that he had created these persons himself.

"In this book," he writes in his last volume (in the magnificent summing up in which he examines himself as the artist who makes and preserves experience) "in this book in which there is not a single personage *à clef*, where I have invented everything to suit the requirements of my presentation . . ."

On first reading this we are tempted to proclaim it an audacious falsehood. Proust writes a novel that can stem only out of his own experience, he names his hero after himself, he tells his story in the first person, and he boldly proclaims—he has written a fiction! Nevertheless as we pursue Proust's meaning we discover that he is stating a fundamental truth. "In writing," he says, ". . . there is not a single invented character to whom he [the author] could not give sixty names of people he has observed, of whom one poses for a grimace, another for an eye-glass, another for his temper, another for a particular movement of the arms." And he adds: "It is the feeling for the general in the potential writer which selects material suitable to a work of art because of its generality." So Henry James pleaded with his brother, his aunt, his close friends, who told him he had cruelly caricatured Miss Peabody of Boston, Hawthorne's sister-in-law, in his portrait of the social reformer in *The Bostonians.* James replied that the character was evolved "entirely from my moral consciousness, like every other person I have ever drawn." She was perhaps a synthesis of several Boston women and we have no reason to doubt the truth of James's assertion. Yet it is interesting to reflect that between the name of the Peabody of life and the Miss Birdseye, of James's fiction, there is a strange resemblance. Is not a bird's eye virtually a peabody? Unconsciously James, seeking a type, may have reproduced an observed character. Both novelists would agree, however, that in the process, within the "moral consciousness," the character was re-created.

Characters in fiction are composites, as most novelists tell us. So too the characters in Proust acquire bits of their biography from Proust himself and from the observed details which his detail-searching mind treasured. But it is interesting to discover that even the celebrated "little phrase," that haunting *moment musical* which weaves its way through the *Temps perdu,* is a composite phrase; for in a letter to Jacques de Lacretelle Proust describes it as an "infinitely mediocre phrase of a Saint-Saëns violin sonata, a musician I don't like" (and so it appeared in *Jean Santeuil*), yet later it is the "Good Friday spell," and when the piano and violin sound like two birds it is the César Franck sonata as played by Georges Enesco; the tremolo reminds him of the prelude to *Lohengrin* but it is also a prelude by Schubert and a piece by Fauré. This use of the composite in Proustian creation will ultimately take another form in the work of Joyce; for there we will find composites of language addressed to the evoking of composite associations.

We see, therefore, that while on the surface in Proust we may speak of the work as autobiography, what he is revealing to us is the complexity of his subject, himself as a complex being and the complexity of the people he knew: that we are all in a sense composites of parents and relations and memories, pastiches of the flesh, resembling now this person and now that; that man is not one but many, and we thus obtain from Proust a sense of the variousness and the depth of experience. In the technical sense Proust is writing autobiographical fiction; in the larger sense he has created a synthesis that is art independent of its creator. In the same way I would say that in *Ulysses*, Joyce's three distinct streams of consciousness, though tributaries of his own stream, stand as independent personalities and not as different facets of James Joyce's personality even though we might, by close searching, say that Molly Bloom expresses a certain part of the feminine in his nature as well as his experience of women and is perhaps a synthesis of all the women he has known, while Bloom has those obsessive qualities which Joyce himself had and revealed in carrying through a work such as *Finnegans Wake.*

For all this, we find in Proust sometimes a deliberate and curious blurring of the dividing line between autobiography and fiction. In Swann he creates a character distinct from the narrator Marcel, in the same sense that Bloom possesses his own striking identity for all that he is a projection of Joyce. In the first part of the *Temps perdu,* Proust introduces what amounts to a separate *nouvelle,* the story of "Swann in Love," which stands out as an almost conventional piece of fiction tied by many visible and invisible threads to the rest of the work. As Proust sets out to tell this story he seems inclined to divorce the narrative from the mind of his narrator. But he cannot bring himself to do so. His intellectual probity tells him that a connecting link remains. And so he analyzes what this process involves.

Swann's affair with Odette, he tells us, had occurred before Marcel was born. Proust, therefore, can only be, so to speak, Swann's biographer. The story was told him, he says, "with that accuracy of detail which it is easier, often, to obtain when we are studying the lives of people who have been dead for centuries than when we are trying to chronicle those of our own most intimate friends." Nevertheless he will not write biography. He draws the story into himself and turns it into part of Marcel's story. For the stories he heard about Swann were condensed, he says, "into a single substance" in his mind, "but had not so far coalesced that I could not discern between the three strata, between my oldest, my instinctive memories, those others, inspired more recently by a taste or 'perfume' and those which were actually the memories of another, from whom I had acquired them at second hand—no fissures, indeed, no geological faults, but at least those veins, those streaks of colour which in certain rocks, in certain marbles, point to differences of origin, age and formation."

This geological analogy, evolved for the grouping of his different memories, is strangely like William James's picture of memory in which he says the "transition between the thought of one object and the thought of another is no more a break in the *thought* than a joint in a bamboo is a break in the wood. It is a part of the *consciousness* as much as the joint is a part of the bamboo." So Swann and the story of his misadventure in love, has become a part of the consciousness of Marcel; and Swann, unlike Bloom, is not projected as separate from Marcel's mind; he remains a layer of memory in the strata of Marcel's mind. But he has a separate identity within that memory.

Memory in Proust, therefore, is not the mere act of recalling events in a given sequence, ordinarily chronological, which is what we usually think of as being autobiography. Proust tries to show us that memory is composite, a process of free association which shuffles events out of sequence like a deck of cards and across great gaps of time, so that we continue to see people as young who have grown old, and to think of people alive who are dead, and recover places and scenes that have changed or vanished altogether. Proust said that "memory, by introducing the past into the present without modification, as though it were the present, eliminates precisely that great Time-dimension in accordance with which life is realised." And this, by its very nature, becomes a synthetic process.

A work of art thus is not just a sum of its parts, that is a sum of things remembered by the artist. A great soldier will set down his memories, in sequence, of battles fought, adventures lived, honors won and personalities encountered and they might make interesting reading, like the sequence of events that fill a daily newspaper. But we do not consider this art. Certainly we can consider it autobiography. These same memories, fused into a synthesis of experience, blended with the texture of life, as the battles are in *War and Peace* or in the historical panorama of *La Chartreuse de Parme,* become a work of art: it is the way the disparate elements have been fused and brought together and the raw material transformed by the illumination of the mind into the work that, beyond its temporal significance, becomes a part of the experience of successive generations of readers.

4

What view did Joyce have of this problem of the artist's relation to his material, he who was so articulate and logical in the creation of his personal esthetic? He has offered us a very cogent statement embodied in the closing pages of *A Portrait of the Artist as a Young Man.* I have already used portions of this passage to illustrate specific points, but now I would like to quote the entire passage:

— . . . The lyrical form is in fact the simplest verbal vesture of an instant of emotion, a rhythmical cry such as ages ago cheered on the man who pulled at the oar or dragged stones up a slope. He who utters it is more conscious of the instant of emotion than of himself as feeling emotion. The simplest epical form is seen emerging out of lyrical litera- ture when the artist prolongs and broods upon himself as the centre of an epical event and this form progresses till the centre of emotional gravity is equidistant from the artist himself and from others. The narrative is no longer purely personal. The personality of the artist passes into the narra- tion itself, flowing round and round the persons and the action like a vital sea. This progress you will see easily in that old English ballad *Turpin Hero,* which begins in the first person and ends in the third person. The dramatic form is reached when the vitality which has flowed and eddied round each person fills every person with such vital force that he or she assumes a proper and intangible esthetic life. The personality of the artist, at first a cry or a cadence or a mood and then a fluid and lambent narrative, finally refines itself out of existence, impersonalizes itself, so to speak. The esthetic image in the dramatic form is life purified in and reprojected from the human imagination. The mystery of esthetic like that of material creation is accomplished. The artist, like the God of creation, remains within or behind or beyond or above his handiwork, invisible, refined out of existence, indifferent, paring his fingernails.

Like Proust, then, Joyce reaches the conclusion that although fictional characters begin in the first person they can end in the third, having taken their vitality from their creator; the creator, theoretically at least, removes himself into the anonymity of a seemingly disinterested spectator. The picture Joyce dresses before us of lyric-epic-dramatic is not unlike the picture he evoked in the Holles Street lying-in hospital where Stephen waits with the medical students for the birth of the child; this episode is told in a parody of English literature proceeding from the infant gurglings of the baby (lyrical), to the sophisticated prose of the nineteenth century. In essence what Joyce is describing, in defining the evolution of the drama from the lyric cry by transition through the epic, is not unlike the picture Freud drew of the stages of man's development, again from the infant cry, lyrical, for milk, to be followed by the growing awareness that milk appeases hunger, and then a further awareness that the breast or bottle which supply the milk are related to other persons, leading to awareness of self in relation to an object or person, which is the general stage at which the infant takes the path of his ultimate adulthood. The artist goes beyond such awareness. He is aware not only of his relationship to the object or person, but *of the awareness of others in their relationship to the object*. When the artist gives a dramatic picture of these relationships and the feelings that are involved in them, he has successfully removed himself within, behind, above or beyond his creation.

I think, however, that Joyce is not quite right in saying that the artist has been, by this process, refined out of existence. The dissociation is not complete. He remains after all within, behind, above or beyond the work—and not too far beyond. He is like those dreams we have in which we are both the actor and the audience: in which we act and also stand by watching ourselves in action. So a work of fiction, if not autobiography of the artist, is still a particular synthesis created by him, and by no one else. We can thus push our inquiry a step further, to what seems to me the inevitable conclusion: that there remains a quality of mind that informs a work, no matter how much the artist has disengaged himself. This cannot be refined away. When James gives us his experience of looking at posters as a boy, the characteristic personality of James is there even as we have Proust's when the little Proust boy studies his posters. When the kind lady of legend handed a certain little musical theme to Brahms and to Grieg it became a Brahms rhapsody in one case and the music of Asa's death in Grieg's *Peer Gynt* suite in the other. In both cases the theme was the same; and yet the Brahms rhapsody would never be taken for a work by Grieg or the Grieg work be considered as written by Brahms. What is the whole history of the novel if not a history of minds, like Balzac's or Flaubert's, Stendhal's or Tolstoy's, Dickens's or James's, Proust's or Joyce's? We are always aware of these minds and their vision which plays from page to page although what they have created is fiction.

Henry James, in his essay on the "Art of Fiction," has admirably expressed this while at the same time showing how observation, added to a rich experience, can perform the synthesis that we call art:

> . . . I remember an English novelist [he writes], a woman of genius, telling me that she was much commended for the impression she had managed to give in one of her tales of the nature and way of life of the French Protestant youth. She had been asked where she learned so much about this recondite being, she had been congratulated on her peculiar opportunities. These opportunities consisted in her having once, in Paris, as she ascended a staircase, passed an open door where, in the household of a *pasteur*, some of the young Protestants were seated at table round

a finished meal. The glimpse made a picture; it lasted only a moment, but that moment was experience. She had got her direct personal impression, and she turned out her type. She knew what youth was, and what Protestantism; she also had the advantage of having seen what it was to be French, so that she converted these ideas into a concrete image and produced a reality. . . . The power to guess the unseen from the seen, to trace the implication of things, to judge the whole piece by the pattern, the condition of feeling life in general so completely that you are well on your way to knowing any particular corner of it—this cluster of gifts may almost be said to constitute experience. . . .

This power to "have the implication of things" and to "guess the unseen from the seen" is what Proust was alluding to when he spoke of the way in which his characters and incidents were composites of experience. Beside the Jamesian passage it is useful to place Browning's discussion of the "subjective" poet in his essay on Shelley, in which he probes the relation between the work of art produced and the mind in which it was fashioned:

Not with the combination of humanity in action, but with the primal elements of humanity he has to do; and he digs where he stands,—preferring to seek them in his own soul as the nearest reflex of that absolute Mind, according to the intuitions of which he desires to perceive and speak. Such a poet does not deal habitually with the picturesque groupings and tempestuous tossings of the forest-trees, but with their roots and fibres naked to the chalk and stone. He does not paint pictures and hang them on the walls, but rather carries them on the retina of his own eyes: we must look deep into his human eyes, to see those pictures on them. He is rather a seer, accordingly, than a fashioner, and what he produces will be less a work than an effluence. That

181

effluence cannot be easily considered in abstraction from his personality—being indeed the very radiance and aroma of his personality, projected from it but not separated . . . readers of his poetry must be readers of his biography also.

What Browning said of the subjective poet can be applied to the subjective novelist; and if, instead of the word "biography" we read "quality of mind"—for this in essence is what he means—we arrive at a vision of the creative process analogous to that of James, Proust and Joyce.

Of the psychological novelists, James Joyce perhaps more than Proust, in *Ulysses* and in *Finnegans Wake*, removed himself farthest from his work. Proust and Dorothy Richardson, much less, inevitably, because of the very way in which they sought to capture subjective experience, through a single consciousness. Proust recognized this when he said that "the great men of letters have never created more than a single work, or rather have never done more than refract through various mediums an identical beauty which they bring into the world." This is not in contradiction with what he also said about his work as fiction. He was recognizing the peculiar quality of mind that pervades each work of literary art, the quality by which we recognize it as the work of that mind and of no other. And this is so even when we have no biography of the creating mind—as in the case of Shakespeare, whom we do not know save as the shadowiest of shadows, but whose mind remains richly present among us. Or even Homer, who is more shadowy still.

X

THE
NOVEL AS POEM

THROUGHOUT OUR INQUIRY INTO THE PSYCHOLOGICAL NOVEL we have been confronted by a paradox. We have observed that the novelists begin as naturalists or realists—and end as symbolists! In their pursuit of shadowy, dancing, flowing thought they invoke prose—and produce poetry! What begins as an attempt to click the mind's shutter and catch the images of outer reality impinging upon it, ends up as an impressionist painting. Perhaps this proves that the dividing line between the artist who wants to use prose to paint his picture and the artist to whom experience can only be rendered as poetry is indeed narrow. Perhaps it proves that the symbolists were the greater realists in recognizing that literature must recreate life, not attempt merely to document it.

The reason for our paradox is not hard to find. The stream-of-consciousness novel approaches the condition of poetry because the writer holds in his hand one medium only with which to create his work. He has words, even as the painter has color and the musician sound. The novelist sets out to use words to render the very iridescence and bloom of life or to frame in syllables the light and the dark moments of memory and feeling. The "word" must paint a picture, or convey the sound of a freight train rushing through the night and through the mind of Molly Bloom; it must remind the reader of a smell or a lost sensation. And it must be so employed by the writer that it conveys to the reader at least some of the feelings he has experienced at the moment he has used it. The word is asked to carry, on shoulders not broad enough, the whole of a writer's experience.

But words, for all their richness and malleability, are curiously rigid. Each word acquires a history, a long history, as the semanticists tell us, and not only a history etymological but a history emotional as well. Words are our language of communication and while we convey general meanings to each other in using them, each word also acquires a special meaning, both for the user and the listener. To the literary artist seeking to catch the atmosphere of the mind, words are a stock-in-trade as difficult to handle as paints are to a painter who would try to depict sound on canvas. A painter may paint a picture of a train rushing through the night in such a way that those of us looking at the picture will, with our inner ear, hear its rushing sound, even though the canvas remains motionless. So the user of words may find syllables to suggest color which only our inner eye will perceive:

> Going and coming, beckoning, signalling, so the light and shadow, which now made the wall grey, now the bananas bright yellow, now made the Strand grey, now made the omnibuses bright yellow, seemed to Septimus Warren Smith lying on the sofa in the sitting-room; watching the

watery gold glow and fade with the astonishing sensibility of some live creature on the roses, on the wall-paper.

Virginia Woolf here asks the reader to imagine a grey wall and a grey Strand, yellow bananas and yellow omnibuses, watery gold glow and roses on wallpaper. Yet even here, with the invoking of exact words representing colors, some readers will imagine primary colors and some will experience different shadings for the yellow of bananas is not necessarily the yellow of an omnibus and the roses on the wallpaper are all the colors of roses—indeed most of us would imagine those roses as red, but some person might think of them as yellow too. What happens to the stream-of-consciousness writer, in using words in this fashion to record emotion and fleeting impression, is inevitable and clearly predictable. We can see it happening in the later novels of Henry James as he pushes more deeply into the minds and feelings of his characters—and *he* is not writing stream of consciousness but catching only the mood or tone of contemplation and reverie. He begins to use increasingly vivid metaphor; as he proceeds the metaphors become elaborate in the extreme, image piled upon image, into vast superstructures. The confirmed artist in prose finds himself functioning as a poet.

This situation had been occupying, for months and months, the very centre of the garden of her life, but it had reared itself there like some strange, tall tower of ivory, or perhaps rather some wonderful, beautiful, but outlandish pagoda, a structure plated with hard, bright porcelain, coloured and figured and adorned, at the over-hanging eaves, with silver

187

bells that tinkled, ever so charmingly, when stirred by chance airs. She had walked round and round it—that was what she felt. . . . The great decorated surface had remained consistently impenetrable and inscrutable. . . .

Or the imagery of the following passage:

> . . . the suggestion as of a creature consciously floating and shining in a warm summer sea, some element of dazzling sapphire and silver, a creature cradled upon depths, buoyant among dangers, in which fear or folly, or sinking otherwise than in play, was impossible. . . . The beauty of her condition was keeping him, at any rate, as he might feel, in sight of the sea, where, though his personal dips were over, the whole thing could shine at him, and the air and the plash and the play become for him too a sensation.

The writer attempting to create the illusion of a mind flowing with thought and image and impression turns to the symbolist poet; he calls upon all the devices of prosody, exploiting the resources of the language in the belief that it is the writer's task to make the word fit the thought, to match the language of the mind and if necessary to invent a language that will render it:

> Look, look, the dusk is growing! My branches lofty are taking root. And my cold cher's gone ashley. Fieluhr? Filou! What age is at? It saon is late. 'Tis endless now senne eye or erewone last saw Waterhouse's clogh. They took it asunder, I hurd thum sigh. When will they reassemble it? O, my back, my back, my bach! I'd want to go to Aches-les-Pains. Pingpong! There's the Belle for Sexaloitez! And Concepta de Send-us-pray! Pang! Wring out the clothes! Wring in the dew! Godavari, vert the showers! And grant thaya grace! Aman. Will we spread them here now? Ay, we will.

Flip! Spread on your bank and I'll spread mine on mine. Flep! It's what I'm doing. Spread!

Or again:

> Teems of times and happy returns. The seim anew. Ordo-
> vico or viricordo. Anna was, Livia is, Plurabelle's to be.
> Northmen's thing made southfolk's place, but howmulty
> plurators made eachone in person? Latin me that, my trinity
> scholard, out of eure sanscreed into oure eryan! *Hircus Civis*
> *Eblanensis!* He had buckgoat paps on him, soft ones for
> orphans. Ho, Lord! Twins of his bosom. Lord save us! And
> ho! Hey? What all men. Hot? His tittering daughters of.
> Whawk?

Howmulty plurators made eachone in person? Howmulty indeed. That sense of plurality and of the multitudinous in things which Joyce experienced was the logical,
the inevitable, the inexorable end-point of the attempt to
make language describe and evoke the texture of the mind.
Beyond a given point inner reality dissolves into what we
have spoken of as halos, fringes, auras of experience, that
can no longer be rendered as continuous narrative, nor
have the sequence, coherence or order which the novelist
of the past tried to give to the novel. What prevails instead
is the condition of poetry in which we catch what Browning spoke of as the "effluence" of the artist's mind. In a
different context, Wordsworth saw poetry as a remembrance of things past, "the spontaneous overflow of powerful feeling . . . recollected in tranquillity" and Coleridge
saw fancy as "memory emancipated from the order of time
and space." "In truth," wrote Proust, "the events of a life
present no interest when they are shorn of all the feeling

189

which makes of them a poem" and he said also "as art exactly recomposes life, an atmosphere of poetry surrounds those truths within ourselves to which we attain." And again, Proust said "metaphor alone can give a sort of eternity to style." He complained that there wasn't a single fine metaphor in the whole of Flaubert!

2

Virginia Woolf was not one of the architects of the stream-of-consciousness novel. She read Joyce, Proust and Dorothy Richardson and absorbed their lesson. Her peculiar contribution to the novel of subjectivity lay in her awareness almost from the first that she could obtain given effects of experience by a constant search for the condition of poetry. The influence of James Joyce upon her is much more profound than is generally believed. Indeed she herself was prompt to seize upon *Ulysses* as a transcendent work long before it was published and only a few chapters had been serialized. She wrote at the time:

Anyone who has read the *Portrait of the Artist as a Young Man* or, what promises to be a far more interesting work, *Ulysses*, now appearing in the *Little Review*, will have hazarded some theory . . . as to Mr. Joyce's intention. On our part, with such a fragment before us, it is hazarded rather than affirmed; but whatever the intention of the whole, there can be no question but that it is of the utmost sincerity and that the result, difficult or unpleasant as we may judge it, is undeniably important. . . . Mr. Joyce . . . is concerned at all costs to reveal the flickerings of that innermost flame which flashes its messages through the brain, and in order to preserve it he disregards with complete courage whatever seems to him adventitious, whether it be probability, or coherence, or any other of those sign-posts which for generations have served to support the imagination of a reader when called upon to imagine what he can neither touch nor see. . . . If we want life itself, here surely we have it.

She was to have reservations about Joyce but these were to be, in effect, afterthoughts. The impression he made on her was powerful. Her first two novels, *The Voyage Out* and *Night and Day* published in 1915 and 1919 were conventional enough. The narrative proceeded in a traditional progression and there was no attempt to go very far into the minds of the characters. There are, however, interesting portents of what is to come (as there are in the short stories in which she was experimenting). In *The Voyage Out* one of the characters observes: "What I want to do in writing novels is very much what you want to do when you play the piano, I expect. We want to find out what's behind things, don't we?—Look at the lights down there scattered about anyhow. Things I feel come to me like lights. . . . I want to combine them. . . . Have you ever seen fireworks that make figures? . . . I want to make figures. . . ."

In this novel a woman looks at a circular, iridescent patch in the river, watching it with fascination and weaving thoughts around it. The patch is like the distant series of lights; it is the pin point of experience, the grain of sand, the mark on the wall around which Virginia Woolf will have the mind accumulate its associations. Her method seems to be a focusing of the mind in this fashion, in the way in which animals and people—and notably in certain

191

types of mental ailments—will look at some pin point with a fascination all-absorbing, unable to tear themselves away from it. Such a focusing occurs in the works of Mrs. Woolf and around this she gives us the cluster of emotion and memory. By this process she achieves a remarkable, shimmering effect of experience. Light, tone, color play through her cadenced works in a constant search for mood and with no attempt to impart an individual character to the style of thought. There is no attempt at portrait painting; rather does she try to evoke a state of feeling by a kind of mental poesy. The same vein of poetry runs through all the minds she creates for us. It is as if she had created a single device or convention, to be applied universally, in the knowledge that the delicacy of her perception, the waves of feeling, will wash over her readers as she washes them over her characters.

This is alike her achievement and its fatal flaw. The bright flame-like vividness of her books creates beautiful illuminated surfaces. There is no tragic depth in them, only the pathos of things lost and outlived, the past irretrievable or retrieved as an ache in the present. And in this she has fused the example of Proust as of Joyce. I think of *Mrs. Dalloway* as a Joycean novel, diluted, and washed and done in beautiful water-color; and *To the Lighthouse* is Proustian in its time sense, but again the medium is a kind of water-color of the emotions.

Like Proust and Joyce, Virginia Woolf clearly expressed her esthetic of fiction. Once she had grasped the lesson of her two great predecessors, she seems to have known exactly how she would apply it. But her definition of fiction is more impressionistic than the carefully evolved analysis Proust made of his métier, or the Aquinian esthetic of Joyce. She adds little to what has been said, and once we divest her ideas of the eloquence in which they are clothed, we find them rather thin and unoriginal. Precisely because it has become one of her most quoted passages, I want to repeat here Virginia Woolf's account of what she believed should be the material of the novel of subjectivity:

> Examine for a moment an ordinary mind on an ordinary day. The mind receives a myriad impressions—trivial, fantastic, evanescent, or engraved with the sharpness of steel. From all sides they come, an incessant shower of innumerable atoms; and as they fall, as they shape themselves into the life of Monday or Tuesday, the accent falls differently from of old; the moment of importance came not here but there; so that if a writer were a free man and not a slave, if he could write what he chose, not what he must, if he could base his work upon his own feeling and not upon convention, there would be no plot, no comedy, no tragedy, no love interest or catastrophe in the accepted style, and perhaps not a single button sewn on as the Bond Street tailors would have it. Life is not a series of gig lamps symmetrically arranged but a luminous halo, a semi-transparent envelope surrounding us from the beginning of consciousness to the end. Is it not the task of the novelist to convey this varying, this unknown and uncircumscribed spirit, whatever aberration or complexity it may display, with as little mixture of the alien and external as possible? We are not pleading merely for courage and sincerity; we are suggesting that the proper stuff of fiction is a little other than custom would have us believe it.

This is very prettily expressed, but I am tempted to suggest that Benjamin Constant said it much more succinctly long before. I translate freely:

> Man's feelings are mixed and confused; they are composed of a multitude of varied impressions which escape observation; and words, always clumsy and too general, may well serve to designate but never to define them. . . .

Virginia Woolf tried to catch the shower of innumerable atoms, the vision of life, the iridescence, the luminous halo. It was her way of circumventing the clumsiness of words. She went on to specify:

> Let us record the atoms as they fall upon the mind in the order in which they fall, let us trace the pattern, however disconnected and incoherent in appearance, which each sight or incident scores upon that consciousness. . . . Any method is right, every method is right, that expresses what we wish to express, if we are writers; that brings us closer to the novelist's intention, if we are readers . . . everything is the proper stuff of fiction, every feeling, every thought, every quality of brain and spirit is drawn upon; no perception comes amiss.

This, however, comes much more closely to describing the writing of Dorothy Richardson than the art of Virginia Woolf. However much Mrs. Woolf might assert the need to record the shower of atoms "in the order in which they fall" she neither accepted that order, nor believed in describing their frequent incoherence. Her method was that of the lyric poet. She was interested in the sharpened image, the moment, the condensed experience. She saw the world around her as if it were a sharp knife cutting its way into her very being.

From James Joyce, Virginia Woolf seems to have obtained a certain sense of *oneness* and the isolation that resides within it: from him she learned how to give meaning to the simultaneity of experience. London is to Mrs. Dalloway what Dublin is to Leopold Bloom. But her London is a canvas background with light cleverly playing over it and, unlike Joyce, her people are distillations of mind and flesh. Clarissa Dalloway's day in London, also a day in June, as in *Ulysses,* begins at nine in the morning and finishes early the next morning. (Indeed in most of Mrs. Woolf's fiction, time is reduced to a few hours so that even in *To the Lighthouse* where a number of years are bridged in the middle passage, "Time Passes," it is but to link two single days at each end of that period.) Clarissa Dalloway walks through London and the people around her form an encircling wave as she goes to Bond Street or strolls along the Green Park while in the midst of the day the big bronze accents of Big Ben remind us of the ticking of mechanical time while we move in and out of Mrs. Dalloway's mind and the minds of the other characters in the story.

The book's structure seems largely to be modeled on the multiple-scened chapter in *Ulysses* which is tied together by the progress of the vice-regal cavalcade through Dublin's streets. We are in many minds in the streets of London. But Mrs. Dalloway's mind, and that of Septimus Warren Smith, hold the center of the book as did those of Bloom and Dedalus in *Ulysses.* The entire inwardness of the book, its limited time-scheme, the use of multiple views, so that we feel we have seen London through many eyes—and so are aware of it through many awarenesses—the glimpsing of certain characters and then the glimpse of them anew through the perceptions of the principal characters—all this becomes a subtle conversion to simpler ends of the Joycean complexities. But if Bloom and Dedalus are a father and son who meet for a brief moment at the end of a long day symbolically, as Odysseus met Telemachus after a lifetime of wanderings, Clarissa Dalloway and Septimus Smith seem to be two facets of the same personality—indeed the projection by Virginia Woolf of two sides of herself. Mrs. Woolf's diary shows that she conceived this novel as an attempt to show "the world seen by the sane and the insane side by side." And we know from her own preface to it that she first intended Septimus to have no existence: it was Clarissa who was to die or to kill herself at the end of her London day and her brilliant party. Finally she envisaged Septimus as a "double" of Clarissa.

But how is he the double—Septimus the insane, Clarissa the sane? What connections, we might ask, unify them? They never actually meet as Bloom and Dedalus did although their paths converge during the day; and it is the doctor of Septimus, the clumsy inept Harley Street psychiatrist, who brings to Clarissa's party the little bit of news that Septimus has committed suicide. The imparting of this bit of information, a mere incident in a big city, remote from Clarissa, plunges her nevertheless into a deep fantasy and identification with the unknown man who is now dead.

> What business had the Bradshaws to talk of death at her party? A young man had killed himself. And they talked of it at her party—the Bradshaws talked of death.

196

So far it is the intrusion of unpleasant reality and Clarissa is hard at work trying to submerge her feelings. Then comes identification:

> He had killed himself—but how? Always her body went through it first, when she was told, suddenly, of an accident; her dress flamed, her body burnt. He had thrown himself from a window. Up had flashed the ground; through him, blundering, bruising, went the rusty spikes. There he lay with a thud, thud, thud in his brain, and then a suffocation of blackness. So she saw it. But why had he done it? And the Bradshaws talked of it at her party!

This is Clarissa whom Peter had described as the "perfect hostess" and whom he had remembered as a girl, "timid, hard; something arrogant; unimaginative; prudish." There was a "coldness," a "woodenness" an "impenetrability" in her. But we know better; we know also that this façade of the perfect hostess submerges the Clarissa who has intuitions and feelings which she can never fully face. It is on the ground of the failure to feel that Clarissa and Septimus are each other's double. Septimus had choked feeling when his friend Evans was killed at his side during the war. He goes through life utterly numbed by this experience.

> He could reason; he could read, Dante, for example, quite easily . . . he could add up his bill; his brain was perfect; it must be the fault of the world then—that he could not feel.

And so these two principal characters dissociate experience constantly from themselves. Both are incapable of establishing a meaningful relationship with the emotional texture of life: Clarissa escapes by giving some slight play to her insights and intuitions, "If you put her in a room with someone, up went her back like a cat's; or she purred . . ." but the façade of the perfect hostess is untouched, the feeling submerged. Septimus escapes by throttling feeling and creating a new world within, filled with private demons and private terrors, from which he can only seek, in the end, the swift obliteration of consciousness.

The whole of the novel conveys poignantly Virginia Woolf's response to Joyce's success in reflecting how, in a big city, people's paths cross and dramas go on within range of dramas, and yet in spite of innumerable points of superficial contact and relation, each drama is isolated and each individual remains locked within walls of private experience. The book's brilliance, as writing and as poetry, lies in the skill with which Mrs. Woolf weaves from one mind into another. Septimus in the park, sees a man walking toward him and suddenly invests him with the aspect of another man and the trauma of his war experience; and suddenly we are in the mind of the other man, Peter, who sees only a rather disturbed-looking Septimus and his anxious wife Rezia, without beginning to know what violent images have been flickering in Septimus' consciousness. This complex inner material could only be rendered by the use of brilliantly evocative prose-poetry. And this novel, and those which Virginia Woolf wrote after it, illustrates admirably the worth of the symbolist method in fiction. We have only to think of a Zola or a George

Moore creating Clarissa after the manner of their naturalist doctrines to understand the difference. Clarissa would emerge as a commonplace woman, the façade described in detail, but no hint of the fascinating and troubled and mysterious personality behind her exterior. Mrs. Woolf extended with remarkable skill and literary virtuosity the creation of a novel that conveys inner experience. She was capable of finding the words that would show the world through her protagonists' minds: and she participated fully in the significant shift of emphasis, inaugurated by Henry James, from the outer social world—as explored by Balzac or the naturalists—to the sensibility with which that outer world is appreciated and felt.

If the general plan, the painting of the environment is a scaling down of Joycean architectonics, the painting of the sensibility tends to be Proustian. And yet there is a significant difference. In Proust the odor of the lilacs is directly felt and explored with subtlety; his feelings well up out of the page and are carefully communicated. In Mrs. Woolf the odor bounces off the flowers and reaches the reader as a sharp, distinct but refracted sensation. One has indeed an effect of the bouncing-off of light and sound throughout the novel from people and objects and against the receiving mind. Proust touches experience directly. Mrs. Woolf's method is refraction, through a kind of high, tense awareness. The poetry is there on every page and always a synthesis—a pulling together of objects and impressions. In addition to Big Ben heard by London and the people immediately around or near Mrs. Dalloway, they

watch an airplane sky-writing. The airplane serves to unify
the city and the people as the vice-regal cavalcade did in
Ulysses:

> Ah, but that aeroplane! Hadn't Mrs. Dempster always
> longed to see foreign parts? She had a nephew, a missionary.
> It soared and shot. She always went on the sea at Margate,
> not out o' sight of land, but she had no patience with women
> who were afraid of water. It swept and fell. Her stomach
> was in her mouth. Up again. There's a fine young fellow
> aboard of it, Mrs. Dempster wagered, and away and away
> it went, fast and fading, away and away the aeroplane shot;
> soaring over Greenwich and all the masts; over the little
> island of grey churches, St. Paul's and the rest till, on either
> side of London, fields spread out and dark brown woods
> where adventurous thrushes hopping boldly, glancing
> quickly, snatched the snail and tapped him on a stone, once,
> twice, thrice.

This is stream-of-consciousness writing after the manner
of Joyce and a fascinating dissociation of experience which
Mrs. Woolf always conveys to us, a matching of incon-
gruities. From the broad skies we are swept across a vast
city—and fixed on a pin point. The world is blotted out;
the eye leaves the plane to catch a predatory thrush
bouncing a snail on a rock. The world can be reduced to
a snail—but a snail can also become a pin point of experience from which the mind moves out into the world. In
"The Mark on the Wall" Virginia Woolf seeks to explain
involuntary association and always with a sense that memory is an invoking of the incongruous. She sees a mark on
the wall. It seems to jut out. It is not entirely circular. It
seems to cast a shadow. Then:

. . . If I ran my finger down that strip of the wall it would, at a certain point, mount and descend a small tumulus, a smooth tumulus like those barrows on the South Downs, which are, they say, either tombs or camps. Of the two I should prefer them to be tombs, desiring melancholy like most English people . . .

and so on, a mark on the wall, a barrow, a tomb, and her daydream continues to take wing like the airplane in the sky over trees, rivers, the Downs, Whitaker's *Almanac,* fields of asphodel until someone standing beside her brings her back to the reality, the room, the newspaper, the mark on the wall, by saying: "All the same, I don't see why we should have a snail on our wall."

3

Virginia Woolf's fiction took its sharp turn immediately after the publication of *Ulysses*. After her first attempt at stream-of-consciousness writing in *Jacob's Room* of 1922 and *Mrs. Dalloway* of 1925 she wrote an essay that sought to define her purpose. It appeared in 1927 in the New York *Herald Tribune* book section. In it she argued that the future of the novel inevitably had to be poetic; and that the fiction-to-come would be written, one gathered, in the way in which Virginia Woolf was writing her novels. The prose would have many of the characteristics of poetry. Poetry had failed to serve the twentieth century as it had the preceding centuries. The poetic novel represented a compromise. "Prose has taken all the dirty work on her own shoulders," Mrs. Woolf wrote, "has answered letters, paid bills, written articles, made speeches, served the needs of business men, shopkeepers, lawyers, soldiers." The compromise, Mrs. Woolf predicted, would be the taking on by fiction of "something of the exaltation of poetry, but much of the ordinariness of prose."

This was written in 1927 before a great poetic novel, perhaps the greatest, was published; indeed it was then only getting well under way and I doubt whether Virginia Woolf had such a work in mind. For that work, *Finnegans Wake,* seems to me to represent the final stage, the terminal point of the novel of subjectivity. After it there seems to be only a retracing of steps, a return to earlier forms, a reworking and perhaps intensification of earlier material. Joyce created it syllable by syllable, a great mass of sound, a long symphonic work. The written words of *Finnegans Wake* tease the intellectual part of our minds by their composite character and their elaborate many-languaged puns. But when we listen to the fragment Joyce recorded we discover the extent to which this book was written with the ear and for the ear even more than for the eye. The eye often stumbles over words that have a haunting beauty when they are read aloud:

> Wait till the honeying of the lune, love! Die eve, little eve, die! We see that wonder in your eye. We'll meet again, we'll part once more. The spot I'll seek if the hour you'll find. My chart shines high where the blue milk's upset. Forgivemequick, I'm going! Bubye! And you, pluck your watch, forgetmenot. Your evenlode. So save to jurna's end! My sights are swimming thicker on me by the shadows to this place. I sow home slowly now by own way, moyvalley way. Towy I too, rathmine.

In *Finnegans Wake* Joyce no longer attempts to give us consciousness but gropes toward that discovery of the condition of sleep that Proust essayed, and toward the rendering of the unconscious. Man is no longer an individual, we feel him in the mass, Here Comes Everybody. The book is a vast symphonic verbal synthesis, an attempt to render the collective mind and the collective unconscious.

THE IMAGE
IN THE MIRROR

IN ESSENCE OURS HAS BEEN AN INQUIRY INTO THE CAPACITY of language to record inner experience and the capacity of the novel form to convey it. We have seen how within the novel, once there is inclusion of large masses of subjective matter, there is an alteration of the temporal and indeed spatial qualities of the fiction. Mechanical time gives way to psychological time; thought is shown in its flowing kinetic state; but the process of recording it results, in reality, in a kind of stasis so that the inner monologue or stream can be said to be *observed* as well as overheard. And the observation is immediate. Since thought does not arrange itself in orderly sequence, the novel of subjectivity often gives an effect of disorder, and different readers, as we have seen, cope with this in different ways. The inattentive reader speedily loses his way. The attentive reader in some ways must teach himself to read the prose fiction as if it were poetry. Such novels—the works of Dorothy Richardson or of Virginia Woolf—belong to that category of fiction of which T. S. Eliot spoke when he said that "only sensibilities trained on poetry can wholly appreciate" them. By this he meant (what we had in the testimony of the two women poets about Dorothy Richardson) that the novel is read not as a time-sequence but as a heterogeneous series of perceptions each catching its moment of intensity without reference to what lies on the succeeding pages, but the entire reading of which conveys a poetic synthesis.

In his lecture on *The Three Voices of Poetry* T. S. Eliot describes how in a given poem we have sometimes the voice of the poet talking to himself, or to nobody; then the voice of the poet may be heard, addressing an audience; while the third voice is that of the poet attempting to create a dramatic character speaking in verse, "when he is saying, not what he would say in his own person, but only what he can say within the limits of one imaginary character addressing another imaginary character." It is this third voice of poetry with which the subjective novel finds itself concerned, the one in which the author tries to disguise his speech so effectively that—like the great actor upon the stage—he becomes someone else.

In the old novels the second voice of Mr. Eliot's definition was always heard: the omniscient author was nearly always present and nearly always addressing an audience. Perhaps, for the purposes of fiction, we can put it in another way: in the old novels we are nearly always seated face to face with the author; it is he who is looking out of the window and telling us the story of what he sees. We can see only that which he tells us he sees, and only that which he wants to describe to us. However much we would like to go and take a look out of the window ourselves we cannot do so, because the omniscient author is occupying the choice seat. But he is so marvelous a story-teller—when he knows what he is doing—that he almost makes us forget he is there, and succeeds in weaving his spell over us so that we feel we are looking, with him, at the world beyond the window. And how much he knows of that world! He knows all the intimate secrets of his characters, and what they are thinking at a given moment, and why they act in certain ways—and often he digresses to give us his own moral reflections and his own judgments of the people to whom he has introduced us.

In the psychological novel the author is nowhere in sight. Suddenly *we* are seated at the window. Somewhere, above, behind, below, out beyond the window the author is busy being a stage-manager and an actor, arranging what we shall see. He tries to give us the illusion constantly that we are experiencing what is happening there; and in the process he asks us to look at all sorts of extraneous things, strange things, as if we were in one of our own dreams in which impossible and implausible events occur: magical transformations, return of episodes and people out of forgotten pasts, masses of geography and history that are part of the common heritage of man, a veritable mental cinema of flashing images often confused and incoherent, often sharply-focused, so that, as before, we forget ourselves and have crossed over the window sill and are ourselves out there amid the confusion, living all that the writer has arranged for us. From being listeners once removed from the scene, we have become actual participants. The effect is to make us use our eyes to see—and to feel what we have seen—rather than rely upon someone else's report of what *he* has seen. When we stop to think about it, we know that all this has been artfully arranged. And we must face the inevitable truth that the extent of our perception will depend in a marked degree upon our own eyes. The artist, in such a case, can never give us a better pair of eyes than we have. He may sometimes give us tinted glasses, but the perception, the pitch of perception and feeling, is ours, and it is undergoing a curious relationship with *his* expression of reality, his expression of feeling, his perception. It may be that in this process the artist makes unprecedented and unreasonable demands upon us as readers. We must recognize, however, that he forces nothing upon us; it rests with us, if we wish, to make the effort to discover whether communication with him is at all possible. It is not always possible, inevitably; and while this may give a reader a sense of frustration and may sometimes be the fault of the artist, generally it must be recognized rather as a failure of the two consciousnesses involved to establish a harmonious relationship. This happens often enough in life; there is no reason why we may not expect it to happen sometimes in our relationship to certain novels that we read.

The psychological novelist may, also, sometimes take us into certain minds where we do not care to remain. This reflects our taste and feeling and is no reflection on the artist. In life we do not exclusively meet persons agreeable to us. Drawing rooms are filled with people with whom we do not care to remain. Withdrawal again is always possible. Both readers and critics who have insistently asked the psychological novelist to mend his ways and revert to old methods and old forms have failed to recognize the collaborative nature of novel-reading. The argument advanced

210

by certain of our less perceptive critics that there was no justification for attempting to discover new techniques to render subjective experience when the traditional mode of narration has so richly served us, is so much an appeal for turning the novel into something rigid and static that it can only be dismissed as puerile.

It is these critics too who have tended to regard the psychological novel as morbid, because it goes into the mind and explores "unhealthy" areas of experience. They often argue that the subjective novel springs from incapacitated persons, Proust and his asthma, Joyce and his near-blindness, Virginia Woolf and her melancholia? Are we being given the abnormal rather than the normal vision of life? Without trying to argue about the word "normal," we can only shrug our shoulders at such failures in critical perception and observe that among the conventional novelists we find also what might be termed "unhealthy" and morbid material, that such material is part of life and that the novelist cannot be legislated into exuding perpetually radiant health and good cheer. We know that the mind at war with itself, and therefore often troubled and sick, can acquire a sharpness of vision that the person enjoying sound health in broad daylight sometimes does not possess. A sense of well-being in a writer does not tend to encourage him to muse upon his fate. The literary artist concerned with broad daylight may not want to look into the dark corners of the night. Indeed he may be too soundly asleep over a good dinner to be able to do so. But a Marcel Proust, lying awake far into the night, achieves his insights with the aid of his insomnia and we

211

are the beneficiaries of his suffering. I think that we are concerned not with the state of health of the artist but the art itself. Morbidity *qua* morbidity is not necessarily art; but morbid elements in art do not necessarily vitiate it.

I have said that the novel of subjectivity represents historically a return to romanticism; but it is not a return to the romantic hero. Marcel, unraveling his life at Combray, Stephen strutting with his ashplant, Bloom eating the kidney in Eccles Street, Molly, submerged in her sexual fantasies—these are hardly the noble, exalted, developed figures of the old novels. Granted we have moved from the open air of Waterloo and the Napoleonic battles on the route to Moscow, into the cork-lined room, the Martello tower, or even the privy in Eccles Street. We touch here on the question whether a figure is diminished in stature because we see it in its more mundane character. It is a little like discussing the actress who has dazzled us on the stage while the lights have played on her and she has embodied radiant youth and beauty, but who in the dressing-room backstage, amid her powders and perfume bottles, with the paint an inch thick on her face, shows her age, and is shorn of all the romance she has created but a few minutes before. Who will deny, however, that the actress performing her dream work before the footlights and the creature of flesh and blood backstage are both parts of reality, and that perhaps to see the actress in her state of confused déshabillé backstage as well as the creator of the dream, is to understand more richly the difference between illusion and reality, between art and life. I am not sure that each in

212

his own way, the romantic hero, so much an expression of his age, so conscious of the palpitations of his heart, so deeply engrossed in his sensibility, is any different from the more deeply subjective Stephen with his agenbite of inwit, or Marcel seeking to recapture the palimpsest quality of memory.

In 1899 in an essay on the future of the novel, never reprinted, Henry James expressed the belief that fiction had a long and rich road before it.

> Man rejoices in an incomparable faculty for presently mutilating and disfiguring any plaything that has helped create for him the illusion of leisure; nevertheless, so long as life retains its power of projecting itself upon his imagination, he will find the novel work off the impression better than anything he knows. Anything better for the purpose has assuredly yet to be discovered. He will give it up only when life itself too thoroughly disagrees with him. Even then, indeed, may fiction not find a second wind, or a fiftieth, in the very portrayal of that collapse? Till the world is an unpeopled void there will be an image in the mirror. What need more immediately concern us, therefore, is the care of seeing that the image shall continue various and vivid. . . . So long as there is a subject to be treated, so long will it depend wholly on the treatment to rekindle the fire.

James was writing in the era when the "image in the mirror" was still literary, that is before photography and its children, the cinema and television, had begun to project images much more elaborate, detailed and "real" than any fictioneer could ever devise. But now that we have lived half a century into the future of which James was writing, it is clear that the novel form has lost none of its vitality. Certainly the techniques evolved by the psychological novelists, by which they penetrated deeper into realities of the mind, have passed into the common currency of fiction and there are signs among the younger writers of further refinement of techniques and a moulding of the stream of consciousness to new uses as well as an integration of it into the older type of narrated fiction. The novelist knows today that in the portrayal of the mind's atmosphere the literary art has achieved what seemed at one time impossible: Proust's observation of himself, Joyce's matching of language to sound and image, Virginia Woolf's use of poetic imagery, Faulkner's bold sally into the consciousness of an idiot—all these represent victories of literature over the seeming anarchy of life, to be cherished and studied and used. The fundamental law that we have found for all art applies here: that so long as there has been synthesis and refinement, an attempt to achieve an artistic vision of experience and of beauty and a constant search for truth, what has been accomplished has added diversity and richness to the literature of our time. Art is never static. It neither accepts conformity nor does it like repetition. When it is reduced to the status of propaganda, it ceases to be art and becomes advertising. Art thrives best on the variousness of life and on a search for new forms and new techniques. Forms outlive their usefulness; are revived; take on new life. Art can flow into the chaos of surrealism and dada and back again into a beauty more formal and disciplined. It seems to have a way of defying rigidities alike of form and of criticism. Of the art

214

we have examined here we can say that the twentieth century novel need not hang its head in shame. The vitality of a Proust and a Joyce will suffice for the second half of this century's fiction even if it should prove utterly barren of innovation.

INDEX